Advances in Contemporary Educational Thought Series

Jonas F. Soltis, Editor

The Cultural Dimensions of
Educational Computing:
Understanding the Non-Neutrality
of Technology
C.A. BOWERS

Power and Criticism:
Poststructural Investigations
in Education
CLEO H. CHERRYHOLMES

The Civic Imperative:
Examining the Need
for Civic Education
RICHARD PRATTE

Responsive Teaching:
An Ecological Approach to
Classroom Patterns of Language,
Culture, and Thought
C.A. BOWERS and DAVID J. FLINDERS

A Critical Theory of Education:
Habermas and Our Children's Future
R.E. YOUNG

Education as a Human Right:
A Theory of Curriculum
and Pedagogy
DONALD VANDENBERG

Education and the Good Life:
Autonomy, Altruism, and the
National Curriculum
JOHN WHITE

The Challenge to Care in Schools:
An Alternative Approach to Education
NEL NODDINGS

A Post-Modern Perspective
on Curriculum
WILLIAM E. DOLL, JR.

Dialogue in Teaching:
Theory and Practice
NICHOLAS C. BURBULES

Detachment and Concern:
Essays in the Philosophy of
Teaching and Teacher Education
MARGRET BUCHMANN and
ROBERT E. FLODEN

The Logic of Imaginative Education:
Reaching Understanding
DICK McCLEARY

Narrative Schooling:
Experimental Learning
and the Transformation
of American Education
RICHARD L. HOPKINS

Ideology, Objectivity, and Education
JOHN WATT

Teachers' Professional
Knowledge Landscapes
D. JEAN CLANDININ and
F. MICHAEL CONNELLY

Reframing Educational Policy:
Democracy, Community, and the
Individual
JOSEPH KAHNE

Civic Virtues and Public Schooling:
Educating Citizens for a Democratic
Society
PATRICIA WHITE

D0829816

CIVIC VIRTUES AND PUBLIC SCHOOLING

Educating Citizens for a Democratic Society

PATRICIA WHITE

TEACHERS COLLEGE PRESS

Teachers College, Columbia University
New York and London

Published by Teachers College Press, 1234 Amsterdam Avenue, New York, NY 10027

Library of Congress Cataloging-in-Publication Data

White, Patricia, 1937–
   Civic virtues and public schooling : educating citizens for a
democratic society / Patricia White.
      p.   cm. — (Advances in contemporary educational thought
series ; v. 17)
   Includes bibliographical references and index.
   ISBN 0-8077-3500-0 (alk. paper). — ISBN 0-8077-3499-3 (pbk. :
alk. paper)
    1. Education, Humanistic.   2. Education—Moral and ethical
aspects.   3. Social ethics—Study and teaching.   I. Title.
II. Series.
LC1011.W48   1996
370'.1—dc20   95-26130

ISBN 0-8077-3499-3 (paper)
ISBN 0-8077-3500-0 (cloth)

Printed on acid-free paper

Manufactured in the United States of America

03 02 01 00 99 98 97 96   8 7 6 5 4 3 2 1

Contents

Foreword, *by Jonas F. Soltis*   vii

Acknowledgments   xi

1 Education and Democratic Dispositions   **1**

2 Hope and Confidence   **8**
Social Hopes   *8*
Confidence, Democracy, and Education   *12*

3 Courage   **16**
What Is Courage?   *16*
Courage and Education for Democracy   *20*
Courage and Democracy in Practice   *25*

4 Self-Respect and Self-Esteem   **26**
Distinguishing Between Self-Respect and Self-Esteem   *26*
Institutions and Self-Respect   *28*
Fostering Self-Respect   *29*
Self-Respect, Self-Esteem and Institutions: Some Tensions   *30*
Problems with Self-Esteem   *32*
Self-Respect, Self-Esteem, and Education   *33*
Self-Esteem, Feeling Good, and Narcissism   *36*

5 Friendship   **38**
Kinds of Friendship   *40*
Why Is Friendship Valuable?   *43*
Fostering Friendship   *46*
Conclusion   *51*

6 Trust   **52**
What Is Trust?   *53*
Personal Trust   *55*

	Trust in Institutions	57
	Trust: The Role of the School	60
7	**Honesty**	**66**
	The Straightforward Cases: Stealing and Lying	66
	Candor	70
	Obstacles to Honesty and Candor	72
	Self-Knowledge and Self-Deception	74
	Honesty and Political Education	75
	Conclusion	76
8	**Decency and Education for Citizenship**	**78**
	The Values of Decency	79
	What Is Decency?	81
	The Expression of Decency	84
	What Is Wrong with Decency?	84
	Democratic Decency and the School	85
9	**Concluding Remarks**	**88**
	References	93
	Index	99
	About the Author	103

Foreword

This is a book about the role teachers and schools can and should play in educating young people to become good citizens in a democratic society. This is not a civics text, however. It is not about government or about civic rights and duties. It is about becoming and being *civil*. It is about the everyday world we all live in and how certain virtues and values of ordinary people stand out as important to the maintenance and flourishing of a democratic ethos in an open, pluralistic society.

Often, when scholars of education try to get at the heart of the matter of understanding what democracy really is, they quote Dewey's famous aphorism, "Democracy is more than a form of government, it is a mode of associated living." Few if any, however, quote the larger passage in which this powerful statement is embedded. I quote from it here at length because it points in a very subtle way to what Patricia White's book is about.

> The devotion of democracy to education is a familiar fact. The superficial explanation is that a government resting upon popular suffrage cannot be successful unless those who elect and who obey their governors are educated. Since a democratic society repudiates the principle of external authority, it must find a substitute in voluntary disposition and interest; these can be created only by education. But there is a deeper explanation. A democracy is more than a form of government; it is primarily a mode of associated living, of conjoint communicated experience. The extension in space of the number of individuals who participate in an interest so that each has to refer his own action to that of others, and to consider the action of others to give point and direction to his own, is equivalent to the breaking down of those barriers of class, race, and national territory which kept men from perceiving the full import of their activity. (Dewey, 1916/ 1963, p. 87)

If democracy is to be taken, as Dewey does, as a form of social life, as a mode of associated living, a venue for conjoint communicated experience, a breaking down of barriers, and a sharing of interests, then the ways people from many different groups, backgrounds, and talents interact helps make a society more or less democratic. And these ways are governed by a set of homely but essential values, virtues, and dispositions acquired from parental and other formal and informal education. In this book, Patricia White begins an exploration of some of the virtues and dispositions that bind people together and underwrite civility and interaction in a democratic way of living together. She treats hope, confidence, courage, self-respect, self-esteem, friendship, trust, honesty, and decency.

Hope in a democratic society is based on the social belief that the openness and freedom of a democracy will allow anyone to become whatever they are capable of being. Confidence in one's ability as well as in the democratic system is necessary to set one's course with courage. Courage is also required to do what is right and just even in a situation that calls for conformity or unreflective obedience. Self-respect can only come if one respects others. Self-esteem provides the motivation and reward for doing well. Friendship is a special form of bonding individuals together and must be based on trust. Trust in the fairness and openness of the democratic system is essential for its functioning. Honesty, too, must be part of a democratic society, and its breach is a signal of democratic decay. Finally, decency is how we treat one another and speaks directly to our beliefs about equality, tolerance, and other democratic values.

White's treatment of these virtues and dispositions is sophisticated. There are downsides to these desirable values that she considers with great skill and sensitivity. She recognizes the complexity and delicateness of adequately describing these amorphous ways of believing and behaving. Her use of literary and everyday examples helps her convey with great imaginative power the meaning of these virtues and dispositions. Her portrayal of the ethical life is an intimate and sensitive one, not the coolly and rationally detached theoretical one usually described by philosophers.

Her treatment roams the globe with examples from the United Kingdom and United States, from Japan and Russia, from France and Scandinavia and a host of other places. But most of all, she helps us to understand in a very deep and reflective way what it means for a school to be democratic, what is required to pass on democratic virtues by way of the manner in which we treat students and structure their schooling.

It is a warm, engaging, and powerful book. It invites the examination of other virtues and dispositions that serve democratic life. There is no doubt that it is an advance in contemporary educational thought and that it points in a new and important direction for further scholarly work. The concept of democratic education is enlarged and enriched. We can never go back to a simple minded view of civic virtues and civic education.

Jonas F. Soltis
Series Editor

Acknowledgments

Chapters 2 through 8 are based on work previously published elsewhere. In all cases they appear here with some modifications, and in some cases they have been substantially reworked. Chapter 2 is based on "Hope, Confidence and Democracy," first published in the *Journal of Philosophy of Education*, Vol. 25, No. 2, 1991, and also translated and reprinted in *Kommunist*, Vol. 12, August 1991. Chapter 3 is a version of "Educating Courageous Citizens," first published in the *Journal of Philosophy of Education*, Vol. 22, No. 1, 1988. Chapter 4 is an extensive reworking of "Self-respect, Self-esteem and the School: A Democratic Perspective on Authority," published in *Teachers College Record*, Vol. 88, No. 1, Fall 1986, and "Racism, Self-esteem and the School," published in *Education for a Pluralist Society: Philosophical Perspectives on the Swann Report*, G. Haydon (Ed.), Bedford Way Paper, Institute of Education University of London, 1987. Chapter 5 is based on "Friendship and Education," from the *Journal of Philosophy of Education*, Vol. 24, No. 1, 1990. Chapter 6 is based on "Trust and Toleration: Some Issues for Education in a Multicultural Democratic Society," first published in John Horton (Ed.), *Liberalism, Multiculturalism and Toleration*, Macmillan, 1993. Chapter 7 is an extended version of "To be Totally Frank. . . . Teaching the Complex Virtue of Honesty," *Proceedings of the American Philosophy of Education Society, 49*, 1993. Chapter 8 is based on "Decency and Education for Citizenship," first published in the *Journal of Moral Education*, Vol. 21, No. 3, 1992. All pieces appear with permission of the original publication.

IT IS A GREAT JOY to have the opportunity to acknowledge here the intellectual support that has made the writing of this book an easier task than it might have been. First, I am very grateful to the participants in seminars at universities and conferences in Canada, Belgium, Britain, Georgia, Holland, and the United States, where various of these chapters first saw the light of day, for their acute comments and thoughtful criticisms. I should also like to thank the anonymous readers of the Teachers College Press for their constructive and helpful comments.

Then there are three more personal debts of gratitude. I owe a very great intellectual debt to R. K. Elliott for many inspirational discussions that broadened and deepened my view of many of the topics of this book. John White, as ever, offered scholarly advice, continual encouragement, and all manner of practical support throughout this venture. Jonas Soltis first gave me the idea of making my work on civic virtues into a book and then patiently but steadily encouraged me in the process of writing it.

Finally I am grateful to Suzanne Chawner-Budden for her advice and technical assistance in preparing the text for the press. I am also indebted to the excellent staff at Teachers College Press, not least for their impressive attention to detail.

CIVIC VIRTUES
AND
PUBLIC SCHOOLING

Educating Citizens
for a Democratic Society

CHAPTER 1

Education and Democratic Dispositions

This book is a contribution to the debate on citizenship and the education of citizens for a democratic society. This is not a new issue in political philosophy or the philosophy of education. The making of citizens has been a focus of discussion since Plato; and specifically democratic citizenship, although its roots stretch back at least to Rousseau, has been a prominent theme in modern philosophy of education since Dewey. But this work has been given a new urgency because countries all over the world are now seeking to establish democratic institutions—multiparty systems, new constitutions embodying bills of rights, legal trade unions—in place of former totalitarian structures and to educate their citizens in the use of these new institutions.

More than 10 years ago I wrote a book which argued that democracy is distinguished by its values—justice, freedom, and respect for personal autonomy—rather than by bits of machinery, like fixed-term governments, free elections, a legal opposition, and free trade unions. The latter, I argued, are not important in themselves and could, and should, be replaced by alternative pieces of machinery if the replacements better embody the relevant values. My argument was not that the procedures of democracy are unimportant or that one set of procedures can very readily be substituted for another: Both these assertions I would regard as false. My claim was rather that democracy is not to be identified with any particular procedure, as it sometimes is—for instance, with majority rule. In any given situation democracy will be best realized by the most appropriate embodiment of the values of freedom, justice, and respect for personal autonomy in that context. This still seems to me to be right as far as it goes. What it fails to recognize, however, is that there is something just as important as constructing institutions that sensitively embody the values of democracy. Institutions have to be worked and used by citizens in the right spirit. Certainly citizens need a very great array of knowledge and skills for life in a democracy (see P. White, 1973), but they also need to be *disposed* to use their knowledge and skills democratically. They need democratic dispositions.

What is it to say that someone has a certain disposition? Kenny sees a disposition, illuminatingly, as "half-way between a capacity and an action" (1992, p. 84). What he is picking out here is that when, for instance, we call someone courageous, we don't mean that she has an innate capacity for courage in common with the rest of the human race, nor need we mean that she is doing something courageous at the moment. A person possessing the disposition of courage, or as we would ordinarily say, a courageous person, does what she judges to be right against her natural inclination toward self-protection *at the appropriate time*. Dispositions are not the same as habits, even though all habits are dispositions.

Dispositions can be of all kinds. People can be disposed to be niggardly, generous, extravagant, cowardly, brave, daring, clear-thinking, optimistic, self-deprecating, and so on. Thus dispositions pick out qualities of mind and qualities of character of both positive and negative kinds, intellectual and moral virtues and vices. Of the vast array of dispositions that make us the people we are, I am mainly concerned here with certain positive dispositions, or virtues, namely, some of those that must inform a flourishing democratic life. Bernard Williams sets out clearly the place of such dispositions in the ethical life:

> All ethical value rests *in* dispositions. Dispositions are basic because the replication of ethical life lies in the replication of dispositions. They are themselves among the objects of ethical evaluation, and are characteristics in virtue of which people themselves are thought to be better or worse. . . . There are important practical consequences of the disposition view, and of the priority that it accords to dispositions. If ethical life is to be preserved, then these dispositions have to be preserved. But equally, if the ethical life that we have is to be effectively criticized and changed, then it can be so only in ways that can be understood as appropriately modifying the dispositions that we have. (1987, p. 64, emphasis in original)

In this study I attempt to argue for, illustrate, and work out the practical educational consequences of this view for some dispositions that inform a flourishing democratic life. In so doing, I draw on some of the recent work in philosophy on dispositions and virtues, particularly that devoted to the exploration of individual virtues by, most prominently, Annette Baier, Alasdair MacIntyre, Martha Nussbaum, Amelie Rorty, and Bernard Williams. Though these writings are concerned very broadly with the nature and development of ethical dispositions, this book puts them to very specific use to illuminate democratic dispositions, that is, dispositions that citizens require if democratic institutions are to flourish. At the same time, however, these dispositions are not closely tied to any particular institutional embodiment of democratic values. Whatever particular democratic institutions are in place, things will go better in the polity if citizens acquire the appropriate democratic dispositions.

It may come as a surprise that the apparently bedrock democratic dispositions of justice, tolerance, and personal autonomy hardly figure in this book. The reason is that these dispositions, taken together, may be seen as definitive of democracy, and there is already a vast body of work (e.g., most prominently, that of Dworkin 1977, 1985; Rawls 1973, 1993; Raz, 1986; Taylor, 1985, Volume II, Part II; Walzer 1983) that seeks to refine our understanding of them and their application in the democratic context. The focus of this study is other dispositions that democrats need but that have to be shaped to take a particular form in a democratic society. These are, in my view, essential elements of citizenship education that have not, it seems to me, so far been given sufficient attention in the growing body of literature on citizenship.

Chapter 2 starts with *hope*, something that all societies need, and particular forms of which, linked to Marxist ideas, were, for instance, stressed in the literature and films of the former Soviet Union. The argument here is not that hopes are some kind of pie in the sky that democracies, particularly if they are mature political structures, can do without, but that democracies need their citizens to cherish certain peculiarly democratic hopes. A similar stance is taken on *social confidence.* Citizens need to feel a certain, preferably unselfconscious but nonetheless robust, social confidence in the values embodied in their society, and here the focus is the precise character of democratic social confidence.

The kind of *courage* democrats need is sketched in Chapter 3, as are the problems for those who seek to develop it. It is argued that developing courage is not something that either teachers or students should directly concentrate on, for this would be a "misdirection of ethical attention" (B. Williams, 1985, p. 11). Rather, what schools should be providing is a well thought-through and carefully crafted broad education for citizenship, with some attention to the probable obstacles in the way of courageous action. This is likely to produce Rorty's (1986) prerequisite for courageous action—competent citizens with confidence in their competence.

Building on this account of courage, Chapter 4 develops an analysis of *democratic self-respect* and examines the tensions between it and other forms of self-respect. Further tensions are then examined between democratic self-respect and *self-esteem.* The school's role in this complex area of crisscrossing forms of self-directed feelings felt by individual students as well as different groups of students, particularly in multicultural democratic societies, is explored in concrete institutional terms.

Friendship, the subject of Chapter 5, might seem at first oddly out of place in a study devoted to democratic dispositions. For what is at issue here is not social solidarity, fraternity, or civic friendship (which might be one way of characterizing the subject of Chapter 8) but the relationship between intimates characterized by the well-wishing and well-doing that is commonly thought of as friendship. It has a central place in a study devoted to democratic dispositions because, in one way, it can be seen as a test of a democratic society. For only a democratic society can truly celebrate friendship in that it can allow that on occasion the values of friendship may trump civic values. Only in a democratic society is Forster's (1976, p. 82) choice between betraying his country and betraying his friend a publicly admissible choice.

Chapter 6 deals with the connected topic of *trust.* An exploration of trust in its personal and social aspects is necessary for understanding both the fundamental bonds between people and the possibility of social institutions in any human society. In a democracy, however, the picture is complicated by the judicious use of distrust, which is built into institutions as a protective device. In this area the school has multiple tasks that, in the nature of things, cut across one another. It needs to sustain, and sometimes create, trust between students as well as in itself, the school, as an institution. As part of its education for citizenship, teachers have to encourage understanding of, and trust in, the political institutions of the wider society and at the same time teach the importance of distrust. These are delicate, necessarily tension-ridden tasks.

Things get no easier for teachers with *honesty,* discussed in Chapter 7. It is not clear that honesty is always the best policy, and thus students will need to learn judgment about when to speak the whole truth, when to speak less than the truth, and when, perhaps, to remain silent. Institutions can also make it more or less easy for their members to be honest in their dealings. The school, therefore, will need to look at its own demands to see how far it might unwittingly be exerting pressure on its members to be less than honest.

Perhaps a suitable epigraph for Chapter 8, on *decency,* might be E. M. Forster's remark made in 1941 during World War II about the qualities which would be needed in the postwar world:

> What it will most need is the negative virtues: not being huffy, touchy, irritable, revengeful. I have lost all faith in positive militant ideals: they can so seldom be carried out without thousands of human beings getting maimed or imprisoned. Phrases like "I will purge this nation," "I will clean up this city" terrify and disgust me. (Forster, 1976, p. 61)

It is very much what Forster terms "the negative virtues" which are emphasized in the discussion of decency—not insisting on one's rights, going the extra mile, and generally having an attitude of goodwill to nonintimates. These are qualities needed in the new millennium, as much as they were in 1945.

Let me now make some general remarks about five threads that run through this aspect of education for citizenship.

First, the major focus is on the *fostering* of courage, honesty, self-respect, and so on in their democratic forms; that is, the focus is on making children into certain sorts of people. This, as the outline above has indicated, is a delicate process that parents begin long before their children enter formal educational institutions. But, from the first school onward, the refinement and development of the distinctively democratic dispositions are also the job of teachers and educational institutions, in partnership with the family. As this study illustrates with literary and real examples, there are no ready formulae. Teachers have to be sensitive to tensions between values; these tensions require difficult decisions that demand the exercise of careful judgment. Looked at in one way, therefore, this can be seen as a book that celebrates the art of the teacher as a reflective practitioner, nowhere more strikingly illustrated than in the process of fostering dispositions.

A second thread running through these chapters, however, makes it clear that the full picture of the shaping of dispositions is not captured by the image of an individual teacher encouraging, persuading, and guiding students to behave in certain ways. The teacher does not work as the isolated Mr. Chips or Miss Jean Brodie of popular mythology. The teacher works as part of an educational community within an institution. And it is the institution of the school that emerges in the following pages as an enormously powerful force in shaping dispositions. It is a sociological truism that the culture of institutions, to a large degree, shapes, for good or ill, the aspirations, habits, and dispositions of those who work in them. The educational point which all the discussions in the following pages emphasize is that schools need to be concerned with the messages their structures give to students. On the one hand, these include undesirable, unwitting messages to some students: "This institution doesn't trust you, respect you, and so on." On the other hand, more positively, institutions need to give thought to their positive corporate efforts to promote and foster democratic dispositions.

Attention has so far been on the broad aspects of the shaping of students as citizens, and this has not allowed a third thread to emerge, namely, that the school is not concerned with a homogeneous student body. The student body of schools is made up of male and female students coming from different religious, ethnic, and cultural backgrounds. The discussions that follow are sensitive to these differences and to the role of teachers, as individuals and as a teaching community, in helping the very different students in their care to find a place and a voice in the democratic polity. Because students come with different values, skills, and self-perceptions, those seeking to educate democrats need to be sensitive to that inheritance.

The discussion so far may have given the impression that this making of democrats, however benign in intention, is fundamentally manipulative. But this is not so. As well as *fostering* dispositions, teachers and schools are concerned, as their students mature, with increasing their *understanding* of them. This is the fourth thread. The aim is to give students some picture of the nature of different dispositions, their place in the ethical life, the tensions between them, how they might be changed over time, and why some people or groups of people might be particularly disposed to think and act in some ways rather than others. This clearly is a broad set of tasks and not one that will be accomplished in one class or even a set of classes. Over time, however, the intention is that the growth of students' understanding about their own and others' dispositions will emancipate them from an unthinking reliance on certain ways of thinking and acting, whether learned in school or elsewhere. (This comes out particularly strongly in the discussions of self-respect and self-esteem.)

Developing democratic dispositions draws on a wide range of knowledge, insights, and skills. Only some of those are philosophical insights. But the fifth thread running through this account is that they are not substitutable. In Indian dishes the proportion of exotic spices to other ingredients is rather small, but the same effect cannot be achieved by adding more cauliflower or more meat in place of the spices. So it is with philosophy of education in teacher education. It is only one ingredient in the whole, but a vital one. To continue the analogy, it does not have to be thrown into the pot first, but, rather, at the appropriate time. Work on democratic dispositions will not usually occur in initial teacher education but rather in in-service education, when teachers already have considerable knowledge of schools, students, family/school relationships, and philosophical insights can illuminate the tasks they face in the way that nothing else can.

The chapters that follow do not have to be read in the order in which they appear, although if they are, a progression through the topics will be apparent. They can, however, be read as self-standing chapters; to aid the use of the book in that way, the interconnections between the topics are highlighted by cross-references.

Finally, this is perhaps the place to make clear that the discussions do not have as their focus ideal students in ideal schools. They deal with students as they are, in schools as we know them. All young people are constantly acquiring and developing dispositions, as their parents and teachers appreciate when they talk about their becoming more responsible or irresponsible, more thoughtful about others' feelings or more selfish, more single-minded about their studies, and so on. The discussions here are intended to support teachers in their professional roles as they, individually and as part of the school community, attempt to foster students' positive qualities and help them to deal with negative ones. The topics that follow are frequently illustrated with brief literary and real-life examples, but I have resisted the temptation to include more or lengthier examples of educational practice, because these will always be specific to a particular context and thus often require so much qualification as to defeat the explanatory purpose they are intended to have. It is my experience, however, that teachers readily bring their professional insight to discussions like these, supplying examples from their own practice and using them to enhance their understanding of the topics and reflect further on possible developments in their practice. This should not be surprising. Teachers, after all, spend much of their time employing insight and experience to tackle intractable problems in moral and citizenship education.

CHAPTER 2

Hope and Confidence

According to a much quoted remark of G. K. Chesterton, "hope is the power of being cheerful in circumstances which we know to be desperate" (1919, p. 159). But perhaps hope has an even more fundamental place in life and in education. One contemporary philosopher, Mary Warnock, writing about the education of the emotions, says: "of all the attributes I would like to see in my children or in my pupils, the attribute of hope would come high, even top, of my list. To lose hope is to lose the capacity to want or desire anything; to lose, in fact, the wish to live" (1986, p. 182).

Within the last decade the world has seen the countries of Eastern Europe moving toward democratic systems for the organization and control of power. In Eastern Europe and the former USSR, free trade unions, free elections, and multiparty systems have come into being and police state surveillance systems have been dismantled. Thus the *procedures* of democracy have been, and are being, steadily put in place. But democracy does not live by procedures alone. As important as procedures are the values underpinning them and the sentiments and dispositions of the citizens implementing the procedures and living by them. Democratic citizens need, for instance, self-respect, self-esteem, and courage, as I shall seek to show. Is hope, too, something that democrats need? Should it even be "the chief goal of education" (Warnock, 1986, p. 183). Or is perhaps social confidence a contender for that position?

SOCIAL HOPES

In our personal lives we all have our hopes—to win the competition, to read the whole of Richardson's *Clarissa* during summer vacation, to get a more fulfilling job. The object of our hopes is some desirable future state of affairs that it is possible for us to attain but on the path to which there are obstacles. There are also, however, what might be termed "social hopes," shared hopes that relate to the future of whole communities and play a key role in structuring the experience of the community's members. Do democrats need such social hopes?

Social hopes are found in Christianity and Marxism. Indeed, the two most detailed recent philosophical treatments of the notion occur in the writings of the Christian philosopher Gabriel Marcel and in the three-volume work of the Marxist Ernst Bloch. The social hopes embodied in classical Marxism and Christianity share the features of our personal, everyday hopes in that they relate to desirable future states in the realization of which there are difficulties, and in addition they are both characterized by a further feature. In both Christianity and classical Marxism, the object of the hope is inevitable. The Kingdom of God will finally be realized; the classless society is historically inevitable. Christian and classical Marxist hope is directed not toward a future that is a bare logical possibility but toward one that is determined. But if the object of hope in these cases is inevitable, why is hope rather than, say, confident expectation appropriate? It is appropriate for Christians because, although the coming of the Kingdom of God may be inevitable, there is a question of whether I shall participate in it. I can only hope for that and trust in God's mercy. With Marxism I hope for the coming of the true classless society sooner rather than later, in my own or my children's lifetime perhaps, because, although inevitable, there are innumerable obstacles in the way, enemies of the people, counterrevolutionary forces of all kinds, threats from foreign states.

In both bodies of doctrine, hope is seen as a powerful emotion. In both cases it can be characterized negatively in terms of what it is not. Having hope is not simply being optimistic or (pace Chesterton) cheerful about the future. Neither is it a calculative matter, a matter of looking at present trends and making a judicious estimate of how things will go. Having hope is not the same as taking a chance or a gamble on future possibilities. Looking at it positively, for Bloch, the person who hopes "has a thrust toward utopia" (Godfrey, 1987, p. 73). At the same time, that person is taking a stance *against* all that is wretched and alienating in the present situation. The corollary of this is that it is possible to live through such conditions in the hope (quite literally) of the future to come. For Marcel, hoping might even be said to determine what is possible, in that *not* to hope may well affect what is possible. Marcel makes a strong connection between hope and action, claiming that hope is "essentially generative of action" (Marcel, 1967, p. 282).

Social hope, then, in Christianity and classical Marxism, plays an important part in the way those who live by those doctrines structure their experience of the world. In Soviet films characters frequently try to hearten others to bear the intolerable burdens of life by encouraging them to have hope in the future. This happens for instance, in Mikhalkov-Konchalovsky's *Asya's Happiness,* a film set on a collective farm. Also, the absence of social hope is often lamented by thinkers on the left. In *Modern Tragedy,* Raymond Williams (1979, p. 208) regrets the "widespread loss of the future," a deep blankness about what a people may want to become. Henry Giroux (1989, p. 66) attacks Richard Rorty for what he sees as his neopragmatist destruction of social hope.

The Christian parallel is starkly presented in Graham Greene's (1971) *The Heart of the Matter,* when Scobie, a Catholic, comes out of confession, unable to repent of his adultery with Helen and perhaps coming to contemplate suicide:

> When he came out of the box it seemed to Scobie that for the first time his footsteps had taken him out of sight of hope. There was no hope anywhere he turned his eyes: the dead figure of the God upon the cross, the plaster Virgin, the hideous stations representing a series of events that had happened a long time ago. It seemed to him that he had only left for his exploration the territory of despair. (p. 222)

And later, talking to Helen:

> "I've given up hope," he said.
> "What do you mean?"
> "I've given up the future. I've damned myself."
> "Don't be so melodramatic," she said. "I don't know what you are talking about. Anyway, you've just told me about the future—the Commissionership."
> "I mean the real future—the future that goes on." (p. 232)

In both traditions loss of hope is a terrible thing, leaving one in the "territory of despair." And loss of hope itself is a matter for guilt, since in the Marxist context it indicates one's lack of commitment and in the Christian context, one's lack of faith. It is not surprising, given the role of hope in Christian beliefs, that acedia is one of the seven deadly sins. For lacking hope, one lacks vital spiritual energy. Everything seems pointless, and one lapses into apathy. And, as for Scobie, the end of that road can only be suicide.

If, then, according to this account, the alternative to hope is misery and despair, it seems that democrats must need social hope. They must need this emotion to pull them out of apathy and give them the energy to work toward a fuller realization of democratic values. But if we are thinking of liberal democracy, it is not clear that liberal democrats *can* entertain the kind of social hope found in the Marxist and Christian traditions. Liberal democracy is not in the business of offering visions of a future to which all citizens are marching if only they can keep their faith in it. For such a view would commit its adherents to a belief in progress toward a single good life that there seems to be no compelling reasons to hold (see, e.g., Kekes, 1989; Nagel, 1979; B. Williams, 1981). For liberal democrats, the future is an open one characterized by value pluralism.

Perhaps, however, if hope is an emotion with such powerful motivating force, it could be argued that we should keep social hope but drop the idea that its object is unitary and its realization inevitable. So far my brief sketch of social hope has focused on its role in Christianity and classical Marxism, where these are necessary features of the notion. This account raises many questions about the nature of hope and what its place might be in human life, both within and outside these doctrines. How exactly is hoping connected with desiring? Can hoping be distinguished from wishful thinking? Is there, as Marcel seems to claim, a necessary connection with action? Is hope always a good thing? What about wicked, spiteful, or irrational hopes? Is the only alternative to hope despair, or is it possible in some way to suspend feeling about the future? I cannot pursue these and other issues here. I shall simply assume without argument, for my present purposes, that it is possible to drop the idea that the object of hope must be unitary and inevitable and to defend a notion of hope where, roughly speaking, to hope is strongly to desire that some desirable state of affairs, which need not be inevitable and is not impossible, but in the path of which there are obstacles, will come to pass. To lose hope is to fall into misery and despair, to believe that, with respect to the object of hope, all is lost.

With this view of hope, can democrats entertain social hopes? It is tempting to say that the social hope of a liberal democracy might be roughly characterized as the hope for the maintenance and fuller realization of a way of life in which everyone has a chance at self-creation to the best of his or her abilities, in conditions of peace and adequate resources, within a framework of the usual civic freedoms. But if we are focusing explicitly on distinctively *democratic* hopes, perhaps we have, as it were, too much filling here. For hopes for wealth and peace are not peculiar to democratic systems. What is distinctive about those systems is a belief in, and desire for, value pluralism that enables self-creation within a framework of civic freedoms. It is the hope that these arrangements will continue and improve which democratic societies have to keep alive in good times and in bad. Particularly in bad economic times, it will not be easy for democratic societies to keep the peculiarly *democratic* hopes alive. There may well be widespread dissatisfaction with the goods and services a new democratic government, beset with a legacy of problems from a former regime, can produce and perhaps insistent pressures for authoritarian solutions. In such a situation the government has to try to keep hope alive in the maintenance and fur-therance of democratic values and institutions—or, at the least, avert despair. It has the broad educational task here (which currently many East European countries are tackling) of presenting an unvarnished pic-ture of present problems to its citizens along with evidence of its deter-mination (e.g., in the form of realistic programs to tackle inflation and reform the bureaucratic infrastructure) to fulfill people's desires for a better quality of life as soon as possible and as far as possible and to make democracy stick.

Planning realistically in this way, and publicizing one's planning, from the present situation toward a future in which the major demo-cratic values will be maintained and perhaps more fully realized should help to foster the vital energy that Warnock sees as the function of hope. That spirit of hope, however, needs to be supported by another attitude if democrats are to maintain and further the realization of democratic values in the life of a community in any part of the world. Having hope in democracy is, I have suggested, to desire that the system of value pluralism that enables self-creation within a framework of civic freedoms will be maintained and developed, but that hope in turn depends on hav-ing the closely related conviction that democratic values are worth main-taining. The attitude I have in mind is the kind of ethical confidence, in this case in the democratic way of life, that Bernard Williams talks about in *Ethics and the Limits of Philosophy* (1985, pp. 170–171). Williams claims that communities in the contemporary world need confidence in the values they live by. Such confidence is not to be confused with an arro-gant dogmatism, nor should it rest on self-deception. Also, it has to be maintained in the face of what Williams sees as the pervasive demand for reflection on values in the world today, and indeed it can draw strength from that reflectiveness. The problem, as Williams sees it, is to determine "what kinds of institutions, upbringing, and public discourse help to foster it" (1985, p. 170).

CONFIDENCE, DEMOCRACY, AND EDUCATION

It is possible to think of societies whose members have possessed ethical confidence. For instance, hierarchical societies have existed whose members were secure in the belief that these arrangements were divinely ordained. In such societies children could be brought up confident that their society, its fundamental values, and their place in it were all the product of the workings of a benevolent deity. Confidence in such a society rested on a solid metaphysical basis. Societies today cannot in good faith, as one might say, rest on such foundations. (A possible exception here is an Islamic society whose members are believers from uncoerced conviction.) Contemporary social hierarchies can only maintain themselves by coercing, or in some way manipulating, consent to their distributions of wealth, power, or status.

Democratic citizens cannot, then, enjoy the metaphysically based confidence that would come from living in a securely based hierarchical society, but they have an alternative. It lies in developing social confidence in those very values that are disruptive of stable hierarchy, those values that cause one to question the justifiability of compelling some to serve the interests of others. It lies in developing confidence in the importance of a concern for the value of each person combined with a reflectiveness about social matters that, directed at hierarchies of power, leads to the unmasking of their attempts to compel assent to social arrangements. Democratic societies frame their social arrangements in the light of these values, and they need to feel a robust confidence in them as the values definitive of democracy.

It is important to emphasize that what I have in mind here is not the self-confidence that is rightly held to be of the first importance for individuals, in education as in all other spheres of life, but *social* confidence. For a society to have social confidence is for its members to be conscious of its major values (though not necessarily self-conscious about them), to think them important (though not necessarily to think *about* them all the time), and to mutually reinforce them implicitly and sometimes explicitly. How implicit or explicit the fostering of confidence needs to be will depend on how deeply rooted democratic values and attitudes are. Where such attitudes and values are beginning to establish, or reestablish, themselves, as in Eastern Europe at the moment, consciousness of them, reflection on them, and conscious attempts to reinforce them will be more prevalent than in societies—say, the Scandinavian ones—where they are part of the taken-for-granted background to life.

How, then, might education promote social confidence in democratic values? Educators, parents, and school staff in any democratic society will, of course, need a reflective understanding of the democratic values of, among other things, respect for persons, personal autonomy, justice, and free inquiry. This will involve seeing them, not as they are sometimes seen, as rather wishy-washy liberal values, but as an indispensable bulwark against social coercion and manipulation. But in school more than this reflective understanding on the part of individuals is required if the school is to use its resources *as an institution* to promote social confidence. The school staff as a whole, not only teachers but support staff as well, need to discuss and frame together whole-school policies that instantiate democratic values and cover all aspects of school life. In due course the school's governors and parents, too, need to be involved in this process. Here the process of policy formulation as well as the resulting policies can promote social confidence. Coming to a common understanding will not necessarily be an easy matter, and considerable compromise and negotiation may be needed. But having reached a common understanding, members of the school community will feel considerable confidence that they have framed a policy which they can all accept and which is appropriate to the particular circumstances of their school community. (See P. White, 1988, for a detailed description of the way in which a whole-school policy was formulated in one school.)

If students are to feel a secure confidence in these values, it will not be a matter of simply devising programs to *teach them about* the virtues of concern for the individual, personal autonomy, justice, and free inquiry; they will need to live in an institution that enshrines and instantiates these values in its every aspect. Whole-school policies therefore need to be framed accordingly. Both the curriculum and the organization of the school will reflect democratic values, but it is the organization that will be the more powerful in producing social confidence in democratic values. This is because the organization will guide students in actually living by these values. For instance, the organization of the school will set the arrangements for furthering individual concerns and projects within a consensual rather than a confrontational framework (on this aspect of school organization, see Andrews, 1989). In every aspect the ethos of the school will be such that students and staff will, in their interactions, mutually reinforce one another in their commitment to democratic values.

It is perhaps not surprising that many countries in Eastern Europe now reestablishing democratic systems see an important place for work on the framing of whole-school policies that reflect democratic values in the initial training and in-service education of teachers and educational administrators. This is not to say that democratic societies elsewhere can do without this; they may simply think they can.

It is not just in school, of course, that social confidence in democratic values can be encouraged. This can occur in the wider community, too. In particular the media, especially newspapers and television, can have a significant effect on shaping attitudes, including those of students. The fact that the media today often promote values antithetical to democracy does not gainsay the possibility of their reinforcing common democratic values. It is no accident that in the revolutions in the countries of

Eastern Europe, television stations and newspapers were usually the first enterprises to be taken over or infiltrated by the new democratic movements. If societies are to be turned around and citizens are confidently to acquire new attitudes and habits, the role of the media in fostering and celebrating those attitudes and habits in the public arena cannot be overestimated.

In a flourishing democratic polity, then, citizens will cherish distinctively democratic hopes and be confident in their democratic values. Engendering that confidence and encouraging people to entertain those hopes will be the task, often pursued in subtle and tacit ways, of educational institutions, in the broadest sense.

CHAPTER 3

Courage

Courage is a virtue, it is often suggested, that we cannot do without. Philippa Foot (1981) says that "nobody can get on well if he lacks courage" (p. 2). Alasdair MacIntyre (1984) sees courage as crucially important in sustaining our concern for individuals, communities, and causes we care about. It is not surprising, therefore, that in that part of the nationally laid-down *Course of Study for Elementary Schools in Japan* concerned with moral education, the promotion of courage appears as an objective. Item 7 reads:

> To love justice and hate injustice, and to act righteously with courage. (UNESCO, 1983, p. 112)

If MacIntyre is correct about the importance of courage in sustaining communities, it seems right to assume, as the Japanese do, that it would be as important in the development and flourishing of democratic communities as in that of any others. If so, questions arise about how this quality of character might be fostered in citizens and what the role of the school and other institutions might be. But these questions presuppose others. What is this apparently important quality? Is it everywhere and always a virtue? Is it even a unitary quality, or are there different sorts of courage? And if there are different sorts, might not some even endanger communities, as Rorty's (1986) analysis of courage suggests? We need to tread carefully. The first step must be to try to establish what this quality is which sustains communities and to attempt to distinguish it from similar but potentially community-threatening qualities.

WHAT IS COURAGE?

A useful focus for this inquiry is an influential contemporary account of courage as a specific virtue that enables people to overcome specific types of obstacles. According to James Wallace (1986), an act, *Y*, is a courageous act if an agent, *A*:

1. Believes that it is dangerous for him or her to do Y
2. Believes that his doing Y is worth the risks it involves
3. Believes that it is possible for him not to do Y

It also has to be the case (4) that the danger that A sees in doing Y is sufficiently formidable that most people would find it difficult in the circumstances to do Y.

Some examples from literature and life, however, raise problems for this account of what constitutes a courageous act. I raise them not to try to show that Wallace's account is flawed and needs to be corrected in specific ways if it is satisfactorily to fit the bill as the definitive account of courage, but rather to suggest that if we are interested in the virtues needed to sustain democracy in the face of danger, we may need to open our minds to a range of qualities that are salient and to bear in mind some important tensions. Let us look at some examples.

A conversation about what constitutes "being brave" in Julian Barnes's (1987) *Staring at the Sun* brings out a tension between conditions (i) and (iv). Tommy Prosser says, on the basis of his experience in the air force in World War II:

> You can do something normal and the other chaps decide you've been brave; or you can think you've put up quite a good show and they don't even mention it. So who decides what being brave is? Them or you? I don't know. I suppose you do in a way, but they do when it comes to gongs and so on. (p. 47)

This is a rather dramatic illustration of two familiar cases. The first is where the person judged to be brave by others says that he was nothing of the sort: He just did what anyone would have done in the circumstances. (This feature of some cases of courage is, I think, important educationally; see below.) The second case is the situation that the person finds threatening and dangerous (and feels he dealt with courageously) but that others tell him is nothing of the sort: Only ninnies find that sort of thing frightening.

The case of Cliffie in Patricia Highsmith's (1977) *Edith's Diary* seems to raise questions about condition (ii). When Cliffie is 11 years old, he jumps off the parapet of a bridge over the river Delaware on Christmas Eve, for no very clear reason, except perhaps to draw attention to himself. He jumps in the darkness into water he can't see, although at a summer camp "he hadn't the courage to jump off a diving board, even when the distance had been much less and he could see what he was jumping into" (p. 39). Some years later, as a young man, he has a bad dream in which he is asked to dive off a diving board at a summer camp and the other boys laugh at him when he refuses. Waking up from the dream, Cliffie remembers the river incident:

> Cliffie remembered jumping off a much higher thing—the bridge—into the Delaware, however, when he was barely eleven. And hadn't that taken guts? How many guys who had laughed at him in the dream had the guts to do that? It had happened, it wasn't one of his fantasies, because once in a while his parents mentioned it, told people about it. Cliffie considered it the most courageous thing he had ever done, maybe the act he was most proud of in his life, up to now. Purposeless? Sure. What had any purpose in life, anyway? (pp. 77–78)

Conditions (i) and (iii) seem to apply to Cliffie, as does (iv). Most people would find it formidable to jump from a bridge into a river on a dark winter's night. Condition (ii), however, causes problems. While it seems to be the case that Cliffie thinks the act is worth the risks it involves, there is the question of whether he is right to see it like this. Is he seeing something as courageous that should properly be seen as reckless, foolhardy, or foolish attention-seeking?

Another case that raises difficulties for this account is what would ordinarily be seen as courage in the face of death—not in the case of some particularly horrific or painful death but in the case of a death like that of old Uncle Leslie in Julian Barnes's (1987) *Staring at the Sun*:

> He had been not just touched, but impressed by Leslie's behaviour on that last visit. He had mentioned his impending death as soon as Gregory arrived, had wrapped it up in a joke, and then talked about other things. He hadn't made it into a farewell, though that was certainly what it was; he hadn't given way to self-pity, or encouraged tears in his visitor. All of which made Leslie's death less upsetting than it might have been. Gregory supposed that Leslie had been, for want of a better word, brave. (p. 134)

If, like his nephew, Gregory, we want to call Uncle Leslie brave, then we have to face the fact that the acts involved in making his nephew feel at ease do not fit conditions (i), (ii), and (iv).

And what of the role of the successful outcome? Many of those endeavors that we unhesitatingly call courageous would have been labeled foolhardy or reckless had their outcomes been different.

Conditions (i) through (iv) also fail to take into account the end for which the dangerous or threatening act is done. As a member of a Mafia gang, I face dangers most people would find formidable. If, as well, I satisfy conditions (i) through (iii), am I courageous?

Conditions (i) through (iv) also tend to favor a popular view that the person who stands up and fights for his or her principles is courageous while the person who seeks to compromise is a coward.

These examples raise a number of questions. (1) Can there be a final authority on whether or not an act is brave? Is there any objectivity in attributions of bravery? (2) What distinguishes the reckless from the brave act? (3) How important is success for bravery? (4) Is the act done for bad ends still a courageous act? (5) Is courage sometimes too narrowly identified with a particular range of behavior?

It is impossible to do justice to all these questions, and related ones to which they give rise, within the scope of a short chapter, but I want at least to provide sketches of answers to them that seem to me to have an important bearing on political education in a democracy.

From the perspective of education in a democracy, then, let me first address questions (4) and (5), because the answers I want to offer here provide us with a framework for a consideration of courage as an important disposition for democrats. As far as (4) is concerned, I want to suggest that in the context of education for democracy we have reason to ignore it. We are not concerned with Nazi generals or Mafia bosses but with people who are acting to defend the values of democracy—values like justice, basic freedoms, openness in government, and fraternity. These we can assume are ethically valuable ends.

In answer to (5), it is useful to employ a distinction of Amelie Oksenberg Rorty (1986), namely, that there are two kinds of courage, traditional courage and courage redefined. For Rorty, traditional courage is a "set of dispositions to overcome fear, to oppose obstacles, to perform difficult or dangerous actions . . . [with] military connotations [of] overcoming and combat" (p. 151). A person who has the disposition of traditional courage is ready to oppose obstacles, to set aside normal fears of pain and harm to achieve a perceived good. The person who has traditional courage as a major disposition will tend to see situations as offering opportunities for confrontation and combat, victory and defeat. From this perspective, compromise will be seen, inevitably, as partial loss: The traditionally courageous are not disposed to cooperate and compromise. On the other hand, Rorty argues:

> There is an aspect of traditional courage that serves us: we require the capacities and traits that enable us to persist in acting well under stress, to endure hardships when following our judgements about what is best is difficult or dangerous. (p. 151)

Therefore, Rorty argues that we need to redefine courage as that set of heterogeneous traits that enable us to act well under stress, against our

natural inclination toward self-protection. Courage is perhaps best regarded as a wide open set of enabling dispositions. In different situations, different dispositions are relevant. Thus courage redefined enables
us to see both the soldier on the battlefield and Uncle Leslie as brave. In
opening up the field in this way, it sets the scene for an examination of
the place of courage in an education for democracy.

COURAGE AND EDUCATION FOR DEMOCRACY

As a preface to a consideration of the remaining questions (1, 2, and
3), and more broadly, to the place of the development of courage in
education for democracy, I want to focus on two examples of courage
in the defense of democratic communities.

The first example, described by John F. Kennedy (1956) in *Profiles
of Courage,* is summarized as follows by Walton (1986) in his impressively
researched book on courage:

> Edmund G. Ross was an obscure Republican senator. When President
> Andrew Johnson had been impeached by every Republican vote in the
> House in 1868, a frenzied trial for his conviction or acquittal began in the
> Senate. In their fervor to depose the Democratic president, the Republi-
> cans pressed ahead, not marshalling good evidence for a fair trial on the
> formal issues on which the impeachment was based . . . [but] through the
> exclusion of evidence, and various forms of pressure, even including at-
> tempted bribery (Kennedy, 1956, p. 113) simply getting the votes required
> for conviction, by any means possible. The Republicans nearly got their
> majority, but in the end the whole outcome depended on one remaining
> uncommitted senator, Ross.
>   At that point, Ross was subjected to an enormous barrage of pres-
> sure to conform. . . . Ross responded that he would vote for the highest
> good of the country according to the dictates of his judgment (Kennedy,
> 1956, p. 117). In a packed Senate, he voted "Not Guilty" and, as a result,
> President Johnson was acquitted.
>   Ross knew this would mean the end of his political career. . . . No-
> body would listen to his justification of his action when he wrote later that
> it was, in his mind, a question of an attempt at partisan rule based on "in-
> sufficient proofs" (Kennedy, 1956, p. 120). History, however, has vindi-
> cated Ross's act, which according to Kennedy (ibid., p. 107), "as a result
> may well have preserved . . . constitutional government in the United
> States." (pp. 122–123)

The second example concerns the case of a policeman, Frank
Serpico, a case also summarized by Walton (1986) and celebrated in the

film *Serpico,* in which Al Pacino played the title role after spending many weeks preparing it with Frank Serpico. Serpico joined the police force in New York with high ideals of the standards he would expect to find in such a public service. He came to see that there was widespread corruption in the police force, not just in one precinct but in all of those in which he worked. He himself managed to avoid bribes and other corrupt practices, saying he didn't want to "get involved," but this became increasingly difficult, particularly when he was transferred to a precinct where payments from professional gamblers were virtually universal and even officers who didn't like the idea were forced to go along with it. Serpico tried many times to report the corruption to senior officers but got nowhere. Meanwhile his fellow officers ridiculed, ostracized, and threatened him. At last Serpico persuaded a senior officer to go with him and break the story to the *New York Times,* and in subsequent trials he testified against fellow officers, who were convicted.

This was not the end of the story. Later, during a drug raid, Serpico was shot in the head and severely wounded. He always wondered if he had been set up. The police department awarded him the Medal of Honor for this incident, but Serpico felt it was absurd that he should be given the award for that reason and not for his courage in reporting corruption.

At this point it is useful to recall question (1) at the end of the previous section. If we consider these examples in the context of a democratic education, perhaps the question of who is the final authority on whether or not an act or stance is brave seems less important. Ross and Serpico may or may not have regarded themselves as brave, and it is possible that others may disagree on this, too. What there is little room for disagreement about, however, is that Ross's determination to arrive at an independent judgment and to act on it, and Serpico's passionate concern to wipe out corruption, are valuable attitudes if a democracy is to flourish. It is these attitudes that should be encouraged. Perhaps we can let questions about when someone can appropriately be called brave drop out of the picture altogether if our goal is to encourage courageous attitudes in students, who are future citizens. But if we do, how confident can we be that in the future such people as Ross and Serpico will ever arise?

Perhaps the answer is not that courage drops out of the picture altogether but that we need to consider who needs to focus on courage and in what way. Educators, we are assuming, are concerned to encourage the development of courageous students as one of their educational objectives in a democracy. How far do they need to consider what courage is and how it might, for instance, be distinguished from recklessness? Students, it is to be hoped, will become courageous. How much do they need to reflect about what might be involved in this? How much do they need to see themselves as becoming brave people?

Let us take students first. If we follow Bernard Williams, perhaps they do not need to focus on courage at all. Perhaps they need to have the disposition but not to reflect on it, at least not on their having it. Williams (1985) has pointed out that the deliberations of those who are courageous are different from those who are not; but the difference is *not* that the courageous think of their acts as brave. Others may see their actions as brave, but they simply talk about what needed to be done. Indeed, it would be a "misdirection of ethical attention" if people did think of themselves as brave, since they would be thinking about how others might regard their actions rather than about what should be done.

What about educators, parents, and teachers? Do they need to focus their attention on the nature of courage? Perhaps not. If, after all, courageous people characteristically say, when reminded of their bravery, that they just did their duty, what anyone would have done in the circumstances, then perhaps educators should simply prepare people to do their duty, in this case to be democratic citizens. As Rorty (1986) puts it:

> The best preparation for courageous action is the preparation for action: competence and confidence in competence. (p. 161)

In the cases of both Ross and Serpico, we see this exemplified. Both deliberated about what needed to be done in the circumstances and did it. Similar, though harrowing, examples are to be found, throughout Primo Levi's (1987) *If This Is a Man*, of people in Auschwitz who, like Steinlauf, refuse to be reduced to beasts and concentrate on living the life of a human being. In Steinlauf's case, this means concentrating on the details of life, continuing to wash in dirty water without soap and to dry oneself on one's jacket, continuing to walk upright, not shuffling or dragging one's feet. In Auschwitz these were acts of silent courage.

If, then, we are interested in encouraging the development of courageous citizens, perhaps we should concentrate on encouraging the development of people who have a love of freedom and justice in their blood, along with a concern for the welfare of others, and who know how to promote and defend those values in the day-to-day life of a democratic society. For parents, teachers, and future citizens, the focus will be on democratic values and attitudes, not on "being brave." In addition, in the context of the person's whole education, there will be some attention to the importance of thinking through and establishing priorties so that one is not deflected from matters of importance by relatively trivial concerns. I indicated in Chapter 1 the array of values, knowledge, skills, and dispositions required by citizens in a democracy. It is worth emphasizing here, though, that for various practical reasons (having to do with the age at which people become enfranchised and the nature of the school as a public institution) the school is the obvious site for political education. In a democracy, political education might be expected to figure prominently both in a national curriculum and in guidelines for the organization and running of schools.

The emphasis, then, that I am suggesting for educators and students should be on commitment to democracy and preparation for dynamic citizenship, rather than on reflection on the nature of courage and on how brave one is. To defend something vigorously and intelligently, one must be knowledgeably committed to it and able to employ relevant skills in its defense. Making a courageous stand always involves making an effort, and being unclear about one's ends is likely to lead to the thought: Is it really worth the effort? The point is an obvious one. I stress it because it seems to me that the official attitude in the United Kingdom toward education for democracy—as reflected, for instance, in National Curriculum Council documents—is not such as to encourage a robust commitment to democratic values.

The priority, then, must be education for democracy, but this still leaves a number of questions. Should students not be encouraged to think about courage at all? Is there no place for a general consideration of what courage is and how it is to be distinguished from recklessness? Won't such considerations necessarily enter into an understanding of literature and the making of historical judgments? How, then, might understanding developed in these ways affect political understanding? Should students actually be discouraged from thinking of themselves as brave? It may be that I can only bring myself to call attention to a racist joke, which seems to have passed unnoticed, by telling myself that it would be cowardly not to speak up. And what about educators? How much attention do they need to give specifically to courage and its development as part of political education? These questions await a more detailed treatment of the place of courage in a political education.

I am not sure how important it is in the context of education for democracy to resolve question (3)—the significance or nonsignificance of success. Those concerned with education for democracy are involved not with correctly affixing the bravery label on individuals but with encouraging commitment to democratic values and attitudes. In this respect, taking the accounts as we have them, the education that Ross and Serpico had was successful. At the very least it did not inhibit them from taking the actions they did. Even if Ross's stand had been mistaken and Serpico's attempt to root out corruption unsuccessful, it would still be the case that they were acting in the spirit of democracy and in defense of democratic values.

The focus on education for democracy goes some way toward coping with the problem raised by (2)—the need to promote courageous rather than reckless acts. Foolhardy and reckless acts are often the result of people acting out a certain image of bravery, as perhaps in Cliffie's case. If the focus is on promoting and defending the democratic life, people are less likely to be tempted to fulfill a picture of themselves as the archetypal brave person who engages in a feat of daring or, in the democratic context, launches into the showy, but often self-defeating, act of confrontation. Instead democrats, having ends like social justice or the protection of basic liberties in mind, will deliberate with some care about how best to achieve their purposes. This is not to say that a democratic education will eliminate recklessness, even in the political arena, but it should act as a counterweight to those impulses that often urge people "to take a stand," "to show them," where this is not the action most likely to achieve democratic purposes. As Kennedy (1956) argues, the bravest thing to do in some circumstances may be to compromise rather than "bravely" stand up for one's principles:

> Compromise need not mean cowardice. Indeed it is frequently the compromisers and conciliators who are faced with the severest tests of political courage as they oppose the extremist views of their constituents. (p. 17)

Again, just as educating people for life as citizens of a democracy will not eliminate recklessness, it will also not remove the need for those occasions when democrats must stand up and be counted. The argument is rather that a democratic education will help people to determine in a thoughtful way what they should do in a given situation to promote or defend democratic values, rather than falling back on stereotypes. There is a place for the Marlon Brando *On the Waterfront* stand, but it is not everywhere or all the time.

To sum up, this initial foray into courage territory, though it has left a number of questions still to be dealt with, has suggested that the educator's task in developing courageous citizens has two aspects. The negative aspect consists in disabusing young people of any beliefs which suggest that courageous actions form a narrowly defined class, restricted to certain sorts of behavior. The positive aspect is concerned with preparing young people for life as democratic citizens by fostering commitment to the values of democracy and encouraging them to reflect on the priority this has in the light of their other concerns, helping them to acquire relevant knowledge through a broad curriculum, and encouraging them to develop the dispositions and skills of democrats dynamically through the experience of life in democratic educational institutions. A specific part of this second aspect will involve helping young people to overcome fears of different kinds that may prevent them from taking a democratic role, such as fear of speaking in groups, fear of admitting ignorance, fear of expressing an unpopular opinion, and so on. This broad account of the democratic dispositions is not the place to expand on these specific (and largely nonphilosophical) aspects of democratic education. In practice, however, they play a large and crucial role in it.

COURAGE AND DEMOCRACY IN PRACTICE

The above summary of what is involved in making courageous democrats seems perhaps a rather vanilla-flavored affair—it seems to be largely a matter of educating people for democracy with some attention to the fears that might inhibit the performance of their democratic role. One is inclined to feel that the making of courageous democrats should make greater demands: It should be something like a moral assault course followed by character-testing maneuvers. There are two points to make here. First, there is certainly more to be said about developing the virtue of courage, as I have indicated. Second, even the necessary preparation I have suggested for the making of courageous citizens may be no small task, if our unpreparedness for it in the United Kingdom is at all typical of other polities that might claim to be democratic.

In the United Kingdom the educational environment is not as congenial to the growth of democratic values and practices as it might be. Research by McGurk (1987) confirmed again widespread political illiteracy among the 16–19 age group, making them, it is claimed, vulnerable to fascism. Again, as earlier researchers had done (see Crick & Porter, 1978), this report called for the introduction of political education into schools. It is not clear, however, that the education for citizenship that is now part of the National Curriculum in England and Wales is at all a robust enough conception of political education for the purpose, as the many trenchant criticisms of its minimalist character—by, among others Carr (1991), Wringe (1992), and McLaughlin (1992)—make clear.

Against this background it is worth recalling Rorty's formula for the best preparation for courageous action—"competence and confidence in competence." Any democratic society that wants the possibility of courageous citizens needs to provide an education that gives its students the necessary democratic competences and resulting confidence.

CHAPTER 4

Self-Respect and Self-Esteem

Democratic communities need independent-minded citizens, willing to stand up for what they believe, able to challenge any incipient emergence of authoritarianism, and quick to act on the infringements of the rights of themselves or others. One criticism of Germany in the 1930s centers on the apparent lack of these qualities in too many of the citizens of the Weimar Republic. Democracies need protesters and whistle-blowers in the best U.S. tradition of democratic dissent. Sometimes such dissent will take courage, but it will always take "competence and confidence in competence," Rorty's (1986, p. 161) description of the best preparation for courageous action. The exploration in Chapter 3 of the task of encouraging citizens to be courageous involved an outline of the kind of political education required for competence. It is now time to look at the other qualities needed for such action and, in particular, at the role of the school as a institution that can inspire or depress its students and staff. For institutions can induce in their members feelings of inadequacy and dependence—the phenomenon of so-called learned helplessness—or they can in some cases make members feel competent and confident.

I want to argue that schools must encourage their students to feel a certain sort of self-respect and a proper self-esteem. In the later stages of their education, they need also to encourage them to reflect more generally on these attitudes.

DISTINGUISHING BETWEEN SELF-RESPECT AND SELF-ESTEEM

John Rawls (1973), in *A Theory of Justice*, argued that self-esteem, or self-respect (he then used the terms interchangeably), was the most important of the primary goods that should be secured to citizens in a democratic society. Subsequently, particularly in light of comments from David Sachs and Lawrence Thomas (see Rawls, 1985, n. 33), Rawls accepted that there are two different values here that need to be distinguished. In *Political Liberalism*, however, Rawls (1993) seems to run the two notions together again in an expanded notion of self-respect that is divided—as my following discussion illustrates—into a self-respect and a self-esteem element.

> The first element is our self-confidence as a fully cooperating member of society rooted in the development and exercise of the two moral powers (and so as possessing an effective sense of justice); the second element is our secure sense of our own value rooted in the conviction that we can carry out a worthwhile plan of life. (1993, p. 319)

This is not the place to develop an extended exegesis and critique of Rawls's 1993 position on this point. Let me, however, offer some reasons for thinking that the notions of self-esteem and self-respect need to be distinguished.

What, then, is self-esteem? People with positive self-esteem have a favorable opinion of themselves. They see themselves, for instance, as having worthwhile ends in view and the necessary dispositions and capacities to pursue them; or as having achieved something worthwhile; or as the possessors of some desirable attribute, like good looks, artistic talent, or descent from a "good family." Those who have low self-esteem may see their ends as unworthy, or valueless, or they may be totally bewildered because there is no order in their life. They may, on the other hand, see themselves as, for example, too unintelligent or too lacking in self-control to carry through a project, however worthy in conception it might be. They may have a poor opinion of themselves, too, because they feel they have accomplished little or nothing of any worth, or because they see themselves as personally unattractive or lacking in social status.

Whether people are correct in these positive and negative judgments is another matter. Someone who thinks she is unintelligent may be mistaken; individuals are not perhaps the final authorities on the worthiness or unworthiness of their own ends. What matters for self-esteem—whether high or low—is that one should *believe* that one is such and such. This is not to imply that it is *all right* for one's self-esteem to be based on any beliefs whatsoever, including false ones. Nor am I implying that a high level of esteem cannot be too high (for a discussion of these points, see the section below on "Problems with Self-Esteem").

What I have said about self-esteem comes very close to the attitude Rawls described in 1973 as having the secure conviction that one's plan of life is worth carrying out and having confidence in one's ability to do so. He argued then that self-esteem, so characterized, will be enhanced if one enjoys political self-government and equal political rights. As Lane

(1982) and Nozick (1974) pointed out, however, the enjoyment of such rights may do little or nothing for one's self-esteem. Even If I value self-government and the democratic political process, the fact that I am allowed to vote and enjoy other political freedoms may not affect my opinion of myself and my abilities. (This is what makes Rawls's apparent attempt to combine self-esteem and self-respect in 1993 in a portmanteau notion of self-respect the more puzzling.) Such political rights are, however, vital for self-respect, my sense of my dignity as a person. At the extreme I may feel no pride in anything I do and yet *have my pride* in the sense that I will object to certain impositions, find things degrading, be indignant when my rights are disregarded. This is in one sense (other senses are explored in the next section) what is involved in having self-respect, and it is this that can be enhanced by political rights.

Self-esteem and self-respect are complex notions that relate differently to citizenship and need to be fostered by the school with careful attention to the possible tensions between them.

INSTITUTIONS AND SELF-RESPECT

Leaving self-esteem aside for the moment, let us look at self-respect and institutional structures.

Self-respect can take different forms. Fundamental is the formal notion of self-respect, which agents enjoy when they are conscious of doing the right thing, that is, acting in ways that conform to values to which they are deeply committed. These values may, for instance, be religious ones, or connected with a local code of honor, or tied to the values of justice, freedom, and autonomy underlying democracy. It is self-respect based on democratic values and the tensions between it and other forms of self-respect that I want to explore in this chapter.

Any institution has a set of rules that constitute the enterprise and demarcate offices and their areas of responsibility. In a democratic society this authority structure will enable members to function as moral persons and preserve their self-respect, given that it is consonant with democratic values. This democratic conception of self-respect is to be distinguished from the kind of self-respect generated in hierarchical systems, where everyone knows their place and their self-respect rests on observing the rights and duties of that place. Democratic self-respect is based on a conception of oneself as a moral person with certain rights, one of which is to be treated as an equal (Dworkin, 1977), and moral responsibility for one's actions. Authority structures in a democratic society, when they are working well, make it possible for individuals to retain a robust sense of self-respect so conceived.

This does not mean, however, that self-respect based on democratic values is entirely dependent on the external social situation in which people find themselves, with the result that people have no self-respect in a political situation that offers them little or none. Dissidents in totalitarian countries, reviled and mistreated by the prevailing political system that they have struggled to try to change in line with democratic values, are certainly entitled to self-respect and may well feel it. The point is that if an authority structure is to be morally acceptable, it must foster people's democratic self-respect and not diminish it or worse.

There are two basic ways in which educational institutions might have regard for their members' democratic self-respect. First, decision-making arrangements should reflect the fact that members are moral persons with rights and responsibilities. The presumption should be that members of the institution have the right to participate in its decision-making processes and thus bear responsibility for institutional arrangements and policies. This is not to say that everyone should have the right to participate in every decision in every part of the organization. There may be good reasons, which justify making exceptions to the general principle, for many decisions to be delegated, but the institution needs to be open about those reasons and to ensure that the delegated body or person is properly monitored. If members cannot participate in decision making and are not told the reason and how the decision-making arrangements are to be monitored, it is not easy to see how an institution can claim to be supporting its members' sense of themselves as responsible people, that is, their sense of democratic self-respect. Second, an institution needs guidelines that prevent discrimination against any of its members. The antiracist and antisexist guidelines and codes of conduct that many educational institutions have currently established are obvious examples of such measures. In this way institutional life concretely embodies for all its members what it is to be regarded as a democratic citizen.

FOSTERING SELF-RESPECT

More than serving as an influential model, however, the school should also actively seek to foster in students a sense of democratic self-respect. This will involve encouraging students to participate in the school's decision-making processes, including the formation of anti-discriminatory guidelines, according to their level of maturity and encouraging them to understand, in large part through their participation, that they have both moral rights and duties.

This will not be an entirely comfortable process, for students or schools, because part of coming to have democratic self-respect is to become vulnerable in two ways. On the one hand, such self-respect can be wounded by others, as when one is treated with contempt or scant regard and feels moral indignation. Teachers will need to be sensitive to both justified and unjustified indignation against perceived institutional onslaughts on self-respect. On the other hand, one's self-respect can be damaged by one's own acts and omissions, and students will have to be helped to come to terms with the experience of shame at their own misdeeds.

Democratic self-respect is likely to flourish most vigorously when all the members of a community are committed to guaranteeing and fostering one another's self-respect. In good times, this should be an implicit attitude; in bad times, institutions may need to offer explicit reminders. Institutions can, then, given the will, provide a structure that fosters members' democratic self-respect.

SELF-RESPECT, SELF-ESTEEM, AND INSTITUTIONS: SOME TENSIONS

Before looking at the way support for democratic self-respect, other forms of self-respect, and self-esteem may be related in institutions, it is useful to make two points. First, as Sachs (1982) points out, self-respect (in any of the particular forms I have indicated) and self-esteem are not necessarily related in the individual. People can have considerable self-respect but low self-esteem and vice versa. Second, self-esteem, as a number of writers note (Nielsen, 1985; Nozick, 1974; Rawls, 1973; Walzer, 1983), can have any number of different sources. A person's good opinion of himself and confidence in his abilities may rest on any number of different bases—occupation, membership of an ethnic or religious group, sporting powers, agile wit, and so on.

Let me offer three examples that illustrate the tensions between democratic self-respect, other kinds of self-respect, and self-esteem.

In a minor British public school featured in a BBC documentary, a student prefaced a remark to the headmaster about some incident in the school with the words, "in a democratic organization . . ." The headmaster began his reply, "But this is not a democratic organization. It is just an ordinary school." This ordinary school could be the setting for my first example. Such a school may deny its students (and perhaps staff, too) democratic self-respect by not treating them as morally responsible people who are expected to contribute, according to their level of maturity, to the school's decision making, and yet offer at least most of them a basis for high self-esteem. The basis for this self-esteem—this generally good opinion of themselves—may come from the knowledge that they are members of an elite group (public school boys, Etonians, Harrovians) or from their academic or sporting success. This differential provision of democratic self-respect and self-esteem is familiar from many autobiographical and semi-autobiographical accounts of British public school life. It may well be that the organizational structures of public schools preserve the kind of hierarchically based self-respect whereby everyone knows his or her place, but that is not *democratic* self-respect. It is not reconcilable with democratic principles.

British public schools tend to pride themselves on producing the nation's leaders in politics, industry, the law, and the armed services, but they can hardly be providing an appropriate educational experience for members of a democratic society if they fall short on the bedrock notion of democratic self-respect. Sadly, the phenomenon of the institution offering high self-esteem but no democratic self-respect is not confined to public schools.

In the second example, the school attempts, through its authority structure, to support the democratic self-respect of all its members. Some students, however, reject the school's authority structure and its explicit and implicit values of personal autonomy and self-respect. They have no wish to acquire the values that cluster around democratic self-respect, since their firmly established value system is a religious one that has no place for those values. Their self-respect derives from living devoutly according to the religious values to which they are committed. They may well derive high esteem from their achievements in the school's academic, musical, or athletic activities, but their attitude toward the school is an instrumental one. They enjoy self-esteem from their proficiency in the activities of the school but reject the democratic framework and the implicit democratic notion of self-respect it offers. This would be the position of people from some religious groups in mainstream education.

Third, there are the students who reject the self-respect that the democratic framework of the school attempts to foster but do not have an alternative kind of self-respect deriving from some more or less well worked-out alternative value position. They also reject the school's value framework because it offers them no acceptable bases for self-esteem. They derive their self-esteem from out-of-school activities—from anything from weight-lifting, to the status given by a part-time job, to being the toughest member of a gang. Into this category fall the students the school is not reaching at all, the dropouts who are not bound to the school in any way.

These three examples illuminate different types of estrangement from the values of the school. The first illustrates the problem posed for a democratic community by an educational institution that fails to have regard for its members' democratic self-respect. It shows, concretely, the need to build up the kind of self-respecting educational community argued for at the beginning of this chapter. The second example of students who, while enjoying the self-esteem offered by the school's activities, reject its democratic framework for self-respect, in favor of a religiously based self-respect, throws the value conflicts faced by some multiethnic and multifaith societies into high relief. It highlights the need to work toward a common framework of values in such societies (see Haydon, 1987; J. White, 1987). The third kind of estrangement is the most radical in that the students in this group are only nominally in the school at all. They are untouched by its values in any positive way. All three examples, but especially the third, raise questions about the school's responsibility for the self-esteem of its students. What, if anything, should the school be doing about its students' self-esteem? Given that self-esteem can have different sources, or bases, should an educational institution attempt to foster some bases rather than others? If so, which?

PROBLEMS WITH SELF-ESTEEM

When self-esteem based on various cruelties and harms to others has been ruled out by basic ethical prohibitions, then it may seem that anything goes. I derive my self-esteem from keeping my little home spick and span; you derive yours from being a highly paid journalist; he derives his from his skill at racing pigeons.

Why should this diversity of bases for self-esteem be a problem? Several commentators have suggested that democratic societies should make a virtue of it. Nozick (1974) recommends increasing the number of dimensions along which people can measure themselves, and Nielsen (1985) agrees, provided that noncompetitive ones are included. Many people, too, have pointed out the need for schools to reassess their curricula from the point of view of the often narrowly academic focus of their offerings (e.g., Hargreaves, 1982; Martin, 1993; O'Hear & White, 1991); and, since doing so would undoubtedly lead to an increase in the possible bases for self-esteem within the school, this might do something for the disaffected students in the third example at the end of the previous section. As things stand, schools employ the general strategy of increasing the dimensions on which people can measure themselves with varying degrees of subtlety. Not just prizes for academic work, but sports trophies, art exhibitions, steel bands: All these can be promoted as possible bases for self-esteem.

There are, however, problems with this. Looked at from the prudential point of view, any basis can suffer the vagaries of changing public esteem. What was highly thought of is no longer so. What, then, happens to the self-esteem of the "ordinary housewife"? Is it possible for the school to foster fashion-proof self-esteem?

There are also ethical difficulties. Should the school be supporting trivial sources of self-esteem so that students have a favorable opinion of themselves? Is it possible to distinguish between fostering students' self-esteem and encouraging vanity? And what about other people? It seems likely that fostering self-esteem may lead students to take a standoffish, self-contained stance toward other people who are not supporters of the local football team or whatever; and at the worst, it may lead students to take highly divisive, bigoted attitudes toward others. Students might enjoy self-esteem, but at the expense of an insulated attitude of indifference to the rest of the community. Teachers, seeing these fiercer forms of self-esteem in members of minority groups and in the majority population, have a problem. Should they attempt to destabilize perhaps the only basis for self-esteem this student has?

To attempt to deal with these questions, we need to take a look at the entire educational process rather than to take a snapshot at any one point.

SELF-RESPECT, SELF-ESTEEM, AND EDUCATION

I have suggested the broad guidelines required if schools are to embody democratic self-respect for members in their organizational structures and actively foster democratic self-respect in their students. These apply in the elementary school as much as in higher education, and the suggestions below about self-esteem need to be seen against this background.

Fostering self-esteem—that is, the view that one has worthwhile ends and the necessary capacities to pursue them—is important in all educational institutions. In the elementary school, self-esteem is a pivotal attribute on which all else depends, and so teachers have to be ingenious in finding ways in which to promote it. Fortunately, at this stage there is so much for children to learn—intellectually, physically, practically, morally—that, given the will, it is not too difficult for the teacher

to find newly acquired knowledge and skills of all kinds and new attitudes to encourage and praise. There is no problem with the fact that
some of these things—like being able to tie one's shoelaces, or knowing
when to apologize and doing it—are, from an adult perspective, slen-
der bases for holding a good opinion of oneself because, at the age of 4
or 7, these are real achievements. Teachers need to be careful, though,
that something is indeed an achievement so as not to patronize the child
by praising something as showing effort when the child has just scribbled
it down in 10 minutes. But thoughtful teachers can find ways of making
children feel that they are competent, well-intentioned people who have
what it takes to accomplish the tasks lying ahead and to become a certain
sort of person. Typically this is what teachers in elementary school do.

In the later stages of education, as well as continuing to encourage
students to believe that they can accomplish worthwhile projects and
become admirable people, the school will seek to give them the intellectual tools with which they can take charge of their lives rather than
being propelled by forces they do not understand. With this in mind,
students will be encouraged to take a reflective attitude toward self-
respect and self-esteem and to gain insight into the network of issues
surrounding these attitudes. Such an exploration includes three broad
tasks.

1. The first involves encouraging understanding of the notions of self-
   respect and self-esteem and their interrelationships. It involves understanding democratic self-respect as something different from other
   kinds of self-respect, particularly those generated in systems where
   everyone knows their place and self-respect lies in enjoying the rights
   and observing the duties of that place. It involves understanding that
   preserving one's democratic self-respect does not require one always
   to insist on one's rights, stand on one's dignity, and refuse to compromise. A ready apology in some ethically uncertain situation, for
   instance, might prevent a potential breach, whereas standing on one's
   rights might widen it. This is certainly in line with democratic self-
   respect. Earlier it may have seemed that democratic self-respect involved instant objections to anything that might be classified as an
   imposition and righteous indignation at rights disregarded. If so, I
   hope I have corrected this misleading impression. An ethically sensitive education will introduce students to the rights associated with
   democratic self-respect as well as the need to appreciate when it is
   ethically appropriate for rights to be waived.
2. As students come to understand some of the relationships among different kinds of self-respect, self-esteem, and authority structures, it

may occur to some, either in theory or in practice, that it is possible to acquire self-esteem from one's position in an authority structure. Education should alert people to the dangers here. Deriving one's self-esteem from one's position or office may lead one to attempt to extend the position for one's own glory or, alternatively, to adopt overly submissive attitudes toward others in the organization to earn their approval. This is not to say that officeholders should not think well of themselves for a job well done; but such an attitude needs to be kept within proper bounds.
3. Helping students to learn to keep self-esteem within proper bounds— that is, an Aristotelian "neither too little nor too much"—is the third task of the school. In the later stages of their education, students should be encouraged to explore the bases of self-esteem. This exploration will have two aspects.

There is, first, a social, public aspect covering knowledge of the way societies work and how, in the broadest terms, people become the people they become. This would be covered in large part in the political education outlined in Chapters 1 and 3, as well as in history and the humanities. It is crucially important for the individual's understanding of how he or she came to be the kind of person he or she is. We all, too easily, fall prey to the myth of total individual uniqueness, which can be very damaging if it leads us to think, for instance, that people's fears, anxieties, and guilt feelings—as well as their achievements and successes— are all matters of individual responsibility. The women's movement over the last few decades has certainly shown the powerful effect of coming to understand how social forces shape our lives. (A classic vignette is provided in Virginia Woolf's *A Room of One's Own*.) This kind of understanding is essential if one is to appreciate how it is, in general, that some social groups enjoy boundless self-esteem, while others do not. In this process, as I have indicated, history, the humanities, and aspects of a broad political education are of primary importance in giving students some grasp of the social roots of their own and others' self-esteem.

Schools need also to be mindful of the fact that they, as institutions, can structurally help to enhance or damage their members' self-esteem. It may be, for instance, that some activities in which members of minority groups do not participate on religious grounds are accorded high status in the school. In its exploration of differential social structural support for self-esteem, therefore, the school should actively encourage its students to examine its own role in this process.

Second, this public social knowledge and the examination of both the wider and more immediate structures in which individuals find themselves need to be complemented by an exploration into the individual's own personal bases of (positive and negative) self-esteem. This will involve individuals in taking a "stepping-back" (Smith, 1985), reflective attitude toward themselves and the bases of their esteem. This process will involve asking, among other things, which of one's bases of self-esteem are more important, and why, and from what perspective. Education needs to encourage this effort at detachment from one's bases of self-esteem if students are not to be in the grip of feelings and attitudes that exert a powerful control over their lives but that they have neither been equipped to understand nor enabled to modify. Looked at in one way, educational development is centrally about being able to assess the worthiness of one's goals and one's ability to meet them. This is the answer to the question at the end of the last section about the desirability of destabilizing children's self-esteem. The teacher is always concerned with the necessary destabilizing job of weaning children away from morally unacceptable forms of self-esteem. But also, in a more positive way, schools should be having what might be called a revisionary effect on the bases of self-esteem, by offering the broadest possibilities for children to find worthy bases for favorable opinions of themselves that at earlier stages could not have entered their consciousness. A typical recognition of this is the comment, "I would never have thought I would be playing in chess tournaments, thinking of doing maths at college . . ."

Also, and certainly not least in importance, being helped to take a reflective attitude toward the roots of self-esteem can provide students with a necessary shield against others' prejudices. Persons in the stigmatized group come to see the way in which others' beliefs and attitudes have entered into their view of themselves. With this insight, they are emancipated from the belief that the view of themselves they have come to hold is the "natural," "reasonable" view.

SELF-ESTEEM, FEELING GOOD, AND NARCISSISM

Let me, finally, try to answer some possible objections to the school's role in fostering the self-esteem of its students.

First, in asking teachers to support and foster students' self-esteem, how much are we simply asking them to provide a kind of "feel-good" therapy? Not at all, I think, for socially and personally the explorations suggested are radical and challenging. Those engaging in them should, on the social level, gain some insight into the need for transparency in a democratic society and some awareness of the ideological shields raised by the powerful; while, on the personal level, they should achieve some awareness of the significance of the connections among honesty, self-deception, and self-esteem. Both sorts of insights are necessary for any considered attempt to initiate changes in personal or social life.

A second objection might be that encouraging students to develop a probing, reflective attitude toward the bases of self-esteem is to recommend an unhealthy self-absorption, even narcissism. This is far from the kind of confidence that democratic citizens need. The last thing the truly confident do, surely, is inspect the roots of their favorable view of themselves. This is possibly true, but we need to bear in mind that the educational aim is not, after all, self-esteem *of any kind whatever*, but self-esteem within proper bounds. To this end, the kind of exploration of self-esteem as a general phenomenon that this chapter has recommended in the later stages of education is hardly a narcissistic pursuit. It may well be, too, that a reflectively thought-through self-esteem is in the end more robustly serviceable than the taken-for-granted variety. It may be the best defense against the vagaries of fashion.

To anticipate another objection, there is certainly no need for this project to be individualistic in another sense. There is every reason for the school's attempt to help its members achieve a reflective attitude toward self-respect and self-esteem to be a collaborative matter to be achieved in a mutually supportive community. For this is an educational policy that can unite members of a pluralistic society. True, grounds of self-respect and bases of self-esteem will differ and may conflict and produce antagonisms. This educational experience, however, offers a chance for students to pursue a common attempt at understanding the interconnected issues here. This is one way in which education can prepare students for the necessary processes of dealing with conflict and arriving at acceptable compromises that living in a pluralist society demands (see Haydon, 1987; Jones, 1987; J. White, 1987). It is also one way of trying to bring the uninterested or disaffected students in the second and third examples given earlier in this chapter into the school community. We do not need to assume, for instance, that democratic self-respect is necessarily incompatible with other (e.g., religiously based) sorts; there is room for a fruitful exploration here. Neither need we assume that there is nothing to be done about those suffering from chronically low self-esteem, as much practical work in schools illustrates (see, e.g., Mosley, 1993; Power, 1993).

In concrete institutional terms (see Fielding 1985 for a pertinent related discussion), this exploration can be the subject of a whole-school policy devoted to the encouragement and development of the democratic self-respect and proper self-esteem of all members of the school community.

CHAPTER 5

Friendship

It is possible to imagine self-respecting citizens enjoying appropriate self-esteem, hope in a democratic future, confidence in their values, and the courage to defend them. With these alone, however, those citizens would suffer a terrible lack, for nothing has been said about friendship. One of the worst things that can happen to you as a child in the playground is to discover that your best friend does not want to play with you, while perhaps the saddest aspect of old age is to be the one who is left. At both ends of life and at all stages in between, Aristotle's view that "without friends no one would choose to live, though he had all other goods" (*Nicomachean Ethics*, 8.1.1154b) seems to capture the value we place on friendship.

If friendship is so valuable to us, does it have a place among the major aims of education in a democracy? Is it the kind of thing that *could* be fostered by education in the broadest sense? If so, is the encouragement of friendship something that could figure among the aims of *school* education? To tackle these questions, we need, first, to have some idea of what friendship is, of what we value in valuing friendship. Is it a unitary thing? When I mentioned to the director of a firm that I was doing some philosophical work on friendship, he replied, "Ah, you mean affiliation." Did he have in mind the same kind of thing as the therapist who recommends that people should have friends because such "well-connected" people live longer and healthier lives (Bellah et al., 1985, p. 135)? Are either of them talking about the same thing as the friendship of Kate and Sue described by Lawrence Blum (1980)?

> Kate and Sue are friends. Both are clerical workers in the same large insurance firm. Sue is a quiet, thoughtful and somewhat moody person; Kate is cheery and outgoing.
>
> Sue and Kate enjoy each other's company. They enjoy talking about people they know and events that take place in the office. They appreciate and value qualities they see in each other. Kate feels she learns a lot from Sue.
>
> Kate cares very much for Sue. Sue has a tendency to get depressed quite often. Kate has learned how to make Sue feel better when she is in such moods. Sue is not naturally or readily open about what is bothering

her; but Kate has learned how to draw her out when she feels that Sue wants to talk. Sometimes she pushes Sue too hard and is rebuffed by her, in a not especially sensitive way. Kate is hurt by such rebuffs. But more often Sue is glad to have such a good friend to talk to, and is grateful for Kate's concern for her, and for Kate's initiative in getting her to talk. Sometimes Kate can cheer Sue up just by being cheerful herself (as she naturally is anyway), but she often senses when such a mood would not be appropriate.

Kate and Sue are comfortable with each other. They feel able to "be themselves" with each other, more so than with most other people. They trust each other and do not feel that they need to "keep up a good front" with one another. The women trust each other with personal matters which they do not usually discuss with their husbands. They know that the other will treat the matter seriously, and will not breach the confidence involved. They know each other well and know how to be helpful to the other in discussing intimate personal matters. They care deeply for each other, and they know this about each other, though they do not express it to each other explicitly. Each one appreciates the care and concern which she knows the other has for her. This is part of what enables them to be so open with each other—the knowledge that the response will be a caring one, even when it is not directly helpful in a practical sense.

Kate and Sue are willing to go to great lengths to help each other out. They readily do favours for each other—helping shop, picking up something at the cleaners, making excuses and covering for each other at work, taking care of each other's children.

When Kate is troubled about something Sue is concerned too; and vice versa. Sue thinks about how to help Kate out. For example, she helps her to think about how to deal with her horrible boss.

The relationship between Sue and Kate was not always so close. They came to know each other gradually. Their different temperaments kept them from taking to each other immediately. In addition, Kate often felt, and sometimes still feels, shut out by Sue's reserve, and her rebuffs. She was anxious to please Sue, to have Sue like her, and this often made her forget her own desires and needs. In her insecurities in the relationship she would also not be able to focus attention on Sue's own needs, feelings and situation. In struggling with Sue, and with herself, to reach a deeper level of commitment, she worked through these insecurities. She was thereby enabled to distinguish more clearly Sue's needs and feelings from her own, to overcome tendencies to distort. (pp. 68–69)

We also need to ask why we think that friendship—whether like that between Kate and Sue or some less deep relationship—is valuable. Is friendship valuable to us for instrumental reasons, even perhaps lofty ones, like its role in the promotion of self-knowledge? Has it, or some forms of it, an intrinsic value? How might the reasons for its value affect its status as an aim of education? Is there a downside to friendship that educators need to take account of?

KINDS OF FRIENDSHIP

A good starting point is Aristotle's discussion of friendship in his major ethical works. As Martha Nussbaum (1986) points out, Aristotle devotes more space to friendship than any other single topic. Aristotle's *philia*, though, seems at first sight a more extensive term than *friendship*, covering, for instance, the relationship of mother and child, husband and wife, and other close family relationships. Its emphasis is on sharing and mutuality. But, on reflection, how much *is* Aristotle's concept significantly broader than our own? The idea of parents and children, husbands and wives being friends is not unfamiliar.

As Gabriel Garcia Marquez (1988) says:

> She discovered with great delight that one does not love one's children just because they are one's children but because of the friendship formed while raising them. (p. 211)

What, then, characterizes these relationships? Certainly not every case in which someone genuinely loves or likes something is a case of *philia*. As Aristotle points out, there are lovers of wine, but clearly it is not friendship that is in question here; and that is the case for two reasons which throw light on the notion of friendship. There is no mutual affection, and the lover of wine does not wish the wine well for its own sake. Friendship seems to involve, as Aristotle suggests in the *Rhetoric* (2.4.1381a), mutual well-wishing and well-doing out of concern for one another, in good times and in bad. We look to friends in times of trouble for support, and we also want to share in our friends' sorrows; we do not want to be spared them (see Wilson, 1987). Hugh Campion, an elderly man in Isobel Colegate's (1988) *Deceits of Time*, sees himself as part of a group of friends, but here mutuality is certainly lacking:

> Hugh's reading had always been to some extent a search for friends; his choice of the biography of the seventeenth-century Lord Falkland was part of the search. He liked the idea of a group of friends, to which in his imagination he could belong. (p. 179)

He had been enthusiastic about the Holland House set, the Bloomsbury Group, and "considered himself more or less in a condition of amitié amoureuse with Lady Wemyss."

> This autumn . . . he was beginning on the Great Tew set. . . . The men who gathered around Lord Falkland at Great Tew seemed so particularly charming, brilliant, careless of worldly advancement, virtuous; if there was anything undesirable about their friendships he had yet to discover it. He was beginning to feel that he knew them a little, though of course being so long ago it was harder to imagine them; still he felt he would have been at home at Great Tew. (p. 180)

The case of Hugh Campion and his "friends" may seem quaint and rather sad (though it is certainly better that he has his Great Tew friends than none at all), and I mention it not in a heavy-handed way, to underline the point about mutuality, but because it has some relevance to education. For Hugh Campion's attitude toward people in books is not uncommon, I guess, among readers. If that is right, what might be the role of literature for young readers' understanding of friendship?

Finally, for a case of friendship, Aristotle claims that there must be mutual *awareness* of the inclinations and good wishes of each for the other. It could be that mutual admiration could exist between people who did not know each other at all, but this would not make them friends. Such feelings existed for sometime, it seems, between Philip Larkin and Barbara Pym. Only when each knew of the other's warm appreciation of their work and kindly feelings toward the other did their friendship begin to develop.

Three broad and different types of relationships, for Aristotle, meet the conditions for friendship. They are distinguished by the basis of the relationship in each case, which can be pleasure, advantage, or character. In a pleasure friendship, the bond between the friends is simply their mutual pleasure-seeking. The friendship of people who enjoy one another's company and some of the same activities may have this kind of pleasure cement. But, when the relationship meets some obstacles, unlike Kate and Sue, the friends will not feel inclined to try to work through these difficulties. Rather, the obstacles will be seen as reasons for a parting of the ways. An advantage friendship could be, for instance, a professional relationship. Two young teachers may share ideas and materials for lessons, let each other know about professionally useful courses, and so on. They may enjoy each other's company and chat over a cup of tea at the end of the day in the staff room, but if one of them moves away to another school, the relationship may just fade away. In a character friendship the bond is the other's character and the good that the other instantiates. Each partner loves the other for what makes the other the person he or she is, with his or her particular attitudes, aspirations, and dispositions. Since the bond is based on the character of the partners, the friendship, like that of Kate and Sue, is likely to endure.

It is important to appreciate that the first two types are not in any sense exploitative relationships. The *basis* for the friendship is pleasure or advantage, but the end, if it is indeed a friendship, is still, as John Cooper (1980) persuasively argues, mutual benefit. Also, the categories are not mutually exclusive. Character friends can find each other fun, as can business associates or fellow professionals linked by the bonds of an advantage friendship.

In talking of friendship as a relationship of mutual well-wishing and well-doing, it is important to bear in mind that friendship has its downside, too. Character friends may be drawn to each other for what each sees in the other, for what makes each the person he or she is, but what attracts them may not be admirable parts of the other's character. The friendship may in fact be based on a pattern of vices that, reinforced in the relationship, are ever more openly and impudently displayed. Where the vices are mild weaknesses of character, the relationship will be one that fuels rather foolish behavior; where the vices are more serious the relationship may become a destructive one that, in the extreme, may lead to the mutual ruin of the partners. Such relationships are mirror images, seen in increasingly distorting mirrors, of that between Kate and Sue. Jane Austen has a number of examples of the foolish end of this spectrum, like the relationship between Marianne and Willoughby in *Sense and Sensibility*. In real life, there have been such relationships as that between Oscar Wilde and Lord Alfred Douglas[1] and between Scott and Zelda Fitzgerald. In these latter cases, it is tempting to think that each partner would have done better, have flourished more, in a different relationship.

There are other aspects, too, to the downside of friendship. For young people, the betrayal that is sometimes involved in friendship, and to which they are especially sensitive, is particularly painful. In a secular world where, for many of us, friends are all we have, this can be an experience of intense misery: We have no friend in Jesus to alleviate the pain.

Tragic conflict is another aspect of the downside of friendship. Far from the Aristotelian conception of a harmonious relationship integrated with one's other responsibilities, it may be that on occasion loyalty to one's friend will overwhelm other obligations. It may lead to painful conflicts, where finally one's love for one's friend may force one, after desperate struggles with oneself, to go against deeply held moral convictions.

---

1. I am grateful to Louise White for this example.

The topic of friendship is a vast one, and in this brief chapter I shall have to set to one side many aspects of it and issues raised by it. I shall not have much to say about sexual relationships on the one hand or, on the other, the kind of less intimate attachments people might have to fellow citizens. There can, however, be no impermeable barrier between these relations—lovers are usually also friends in one or more of the senses outlined, and the relations between fellow workers and members of the same community can turn into friendship, as in the case of Kate and Sue. I also cannot consider here a number of questions that this treatment raises: Does it make sense to talk of degrees of friendship? What is the relationship between friendship and intimacy? Do the Aristotelian categories capture all the main kinds of friendship? What, for instance, of friends brought together by a practice like philosophy? In concentrating, however, on intimate relationships of mutual well-wishing and well-doing between pairs or small groups of people, I am still working on a large canvas where I am aware that I do less than justice even to the main features of my subject.

WHY IS FRIENDSHIP VALUABLE?

Both pleasure and advantage friendships obviously have value. What of character friendships? Aristotle and later writers offer a number of reasons for their value. Let me indicate what seem to me to be the major ones.

A value that many people would, like Francis Bacon, see as the first "fruit of friendship" is the sharing of times of joy and sorrow. For this "redoubleth joys, and cutteth griefs in halfs" (Bacon, ed. 1985, p. 141), as the story of Kate and Sue very clearly exemplifies.

Linked to this first fruit is the idea of the friend as a powerful resource. Bacon, echoing Aristotle (*Nicomachean Ethics*, 8.1.1155a) and acknowledging that he is following the ancients, points out that "a friend is another himself" (p. 144). There are many things that a person cannot do for himself either because he is physically unable to (for instance, carry out a wish after his death) or because it would not be seemly for him to (for instance, indicate his merits), and here a friend can take his place.

Another fruit of friendship for Bacon is that "it maketh daylight in the understanding" (p. 142). It does this, according to Bacon, in two ways. First, in having to marshal our thoughts to put our problems to our friends, we actually become clearer about the issues and, as a result, wiser. We enjoy this first benefit even if our friends are not able to give us any actual advice. In the best cases, however, our friends will be able to give us advice on moral and also general practical (e.g., business) matters. In the moral case this is invaluable, since such advice cannot be gotten from books and, given in the wrong way, it can often be wounding and hard to accept; a friend may therefore be the best person to help us avert moral disaster. In this Bacon follows Aristotle, who similarly extols the value of friendship in providing moral guidance (*Nicomachean Ethics* 9.12.1172a). In practical matters, too, a friend's advice is likely to be highly reliable: It will be in one's interest and not twisted to some other end, and also, because a friend will be intimately acquainted with one's situation, it will take into account all aspects of that situation. In this latter respect, it will contrast favorably with advice given by someone not well acquainted with one who may well suggest something that will "cure the disease but kill the patient."

More generally, friendship can simply make things go better. At work, for instance, colleagues may not get on badly and relationships between them may be reasonably congenial, but the situation will be transformed if they are real friends. Working with friends can bring all kinds of satisfactions to the experience of going to work, as well as benefits to the enterprise in which the people are working, as Aristotle noted in his remarks on shared activities (*Nicomachean Ethics*, 9.9.1169–1170b). It might be objected that it will not necessarily be good for the enterprise: The demands of friendship may conflict with the demands of work. In school, for instance, teachers may break up groups of friends because they disrupt their own and others' learning. Often in such situations the value of friendship is sacrificed, and without any great misgivings, to the demands of work. It may be, however, as I shall suggest below, that greater efforts should be made, and should be seen to be made, to accommodate both demands.

Friendship can enrich one's life in a less immediately obvious way. One of the worst things that can happen to a person is for a friend to die. Indeed, it is even sometimes recommended that people should attach themselves to more permanent objects, like the pursuit of truth, so that they avoid the pain of losing loved friends. But some people—for instance, Cicero—would claim that the enrichment of life that comes from friendship does not end with the death of a friend. As Cicero (1971) puts it:

> And may I attempt an even more difficult concept? Even [when] a friend is dead, he is still alive. He is alive because his friends still cherish him, and remember him, and long for him. This means that there is happiness even in his death—he ennobles the existences of those who are left behind. (Cicero, trans. 1971, p. 189)

In several important ways friendship with the dead is continuous with friendship with the living. In both there are loyalty, memories of times spent together, and the sharing in imagination of thoughts and perceptions of events. The pleasure that older people find in reminiscence often involves the pleasure, tinged with sadder elements, of reliving the vivid experience of friendship with friends now dead.

A further benefit of friendship mentioned by Aristotle (*Magna Moralia*, 2.15.1213a) is the increase in self-knowledge that an intimate relationship with a friend can bring. Aristotle suggests that it may be hard for us to assess our aspirations and commitments without bias, but if we see some of our own attitudes and desires mirrored in our best friend, we shall be able to consider them more dispassionately. It may be, too, that our friends will help us more directly to self-knowledge with comments on our attitudes and perhaps lifestyle that it would be impertinent, or at least out of place, for a stranger, or even an acquaintance, to make.

The reasons for friendship discussed so far all cite the fruits of friendship, as Bacon calls them. If we want support when we are in trouble, practical help, sound advice, self-knowledge, and so on, we have a reason to make friends. Suppose, however, our ideal is the self-sufficient, independent life in which one relies on one's own resources. In this case will friendship—the intimate relationship of mutual well-wishing and well-doing—have any value for us? It seems to me that the only answer to be given to the fiercely independent person who is sceptical about the value of friendship is the answer that Aristotle gives. He asks a person who has all the other goods to reflect on what she would be giving up in not having friends. In the passage in which he considers this, he emphasises several times how *strange* it would be not to value friendship. He says:

> But it seems strange, when one assigns all good things to the happy man, not to assign friends, who are thought the greatest of external goods. . . . Surely it is strange, too, to make the blessed man a solitary; for no one would choose to possess all good things on condition of being alone. . . . And plainly it is better to spend [one's] days with friends and good men than with strangers or any chance persons. (*Nicomachean Ethics* 9.9.1169b)

There is no knock-down argument to convince someone who sees no value in friendship that she is wrong. One can only make the kind of appeal that Aristotle does, an appeal that may in fact be made more successfully in a literary work than in a piece of philosophy. One can only *show* the place of friendship in our lives, showing the goods that come to us through our attachments to others and, as a counterpoint, what we lose in living the solitary life. But this bare statement only illustrates all too graphically the need for literature to come in where the power of philosophy runs out.

Where does this leave educators? Should parents and teachers perhaps soft-pedal friendship, since they cannot provide watertight arguments as to why it should have a place in any human life? This conclusion does not follow, I think, for reasons connected with those John White and I have suggested elsewhere for highlighting shared activities in education (J. White & White, 1986). What would be the rationale for underplaying the value of friendship? It should not be concern about what I earlier called the downside of friendship, since most of our values have their negative aspects. However, we do not try to omit these values from, or play them down in, children's upbringing; rather, we educate them to cope with those aspects. It would only make sense to play down friendship if we knew that almost all children were going to be determined loners or Nietzschean *Übermenschen* who might furthermore actually be *harmed* if they were educated in an atmosphere that fostered and celebrated the ties of friendship. As things are, it would be strange, to echo Aristotle, to bring up children in a way that did not acknowledge the very large place friendship has in the lives of most people.

FOSTERING FRIENDSHIP

How can educators, both teachers and parents, encourage friendship? I am still thinking here not of the friendliness and cooperative atmosphere that any teacher will want to encourage in a classroom, but of friendship—the relationship of mutual well-wishing and well-doing between people—in Malamud's (1968) words, the steak, not the spam: "Levin wanted friendship and got friendliness; he wanted steak and they offered spam" (p. 111).

First and foremost, teachers and parents can do their best to create conditions in which friendship can flourish. For parents of young children this means, in the early years, providing opportunities for their children to make friends. It means, too, taking their children's friendships seriously, helping them to keep the promises they make to their friends, and indicating and reinforcing the kind of behavior characteristic of friendship ("Yes, that's right; share it with your friend"). Later it may mean that parents respect the privacy of a friendship. It seems to be important to the notion of friendship that there are matters which are private between friends. These private matters seem to be at least of symbolic importance, marking the closeness of the bond. Friends often say, "I'm not telling everybody but I would like you to know . . ." People also can become quite worried if a piece of information about them becomes public knowledge before they have told their friends. I would like to explore further the role of privacy in friendship. If it has something like the significance I have indicated, however, it is important for parents to recognize the significance of privacy in friendship and not press their children, however subtly, for details of their conversations with, and letters from, friends.

What might be the role of the school in creating the conditions for friendship to flourish? In the first place, this seems to me to require that all staff consider what might constitute making space for friendship in their particular context. Here the elementary school will make different demands from the high school. What will be common to both, and to all other educational institutions, is that in making space for friendship an institution will be implicitly supporting many aspects of the education of its students to which it is already committed. For, as we have seen, friends can provide moral advice, support us in our projects, and help us to develop self-knowledge, so fostering friendships will dovetail with a number of the school's other aims.

If the aim of the school is to celebrate friendship as one of the most cherished of human values, it first has to *refrain* from doing certain things. It has to respect friendship and *show* that it does so in its practices. This will mean, for instance, that teachers will need to consider carefully before splitting up friends. In general, presumably they will want to avoid it by finding other ways around the problem that the splitting up of the friends is intended to solve. Sometimes, however, there will be compelling reasons for such a strategy, for instance, where a pair of students is particularly disruptive of their own and others' learning and a number of other solutions have been tried and have failed. If friends have to be separated, though, this should be done with manifest regret— because it is a matter for regret if an important value has to be overridden for whatever compelling reason—and certainly not with the sense of satisfaction a general might have in routing the enemy.

In Michael Carson's (1989) *Sucking Sherbert Lemons*, Novvy, the Novice Master, has to discuss in his class with the novices an item in the Rule Book of the Order that he confesses he does not like dealing with—Particular Friendships. The Rule runs as follows:

> Particular friendships between the Brothers are to be discouraged because they tend to erode the spirit of Universal Brotherly Love which should prevail in all communities of the Order. (p. 115)

In the world of the Order there is a rationale for the Rule, as Novvy explains. Particular friendships could interfere with the quest to become one with Christ, and they could take away from the love a Brother owes to all the other Brothers. Leaving aside friendships that are woven around the vices, or weaknesses, of the partners to their detriment, it is not clear that in the secular world of the school there is any need to try to restrain or prevent Particular Friendships. Yet from anecdotal evidence, it seems that some teachers feel that they have to put pressure on particularly close friends to "join in more with the others," "to join a group." Devotion to one or two people, however, seems in itself morally desirable, in that it involves, as Blum points out (1980, p. 80), in varying measure and at different times, sympathy, compassion, concern for others, patience, and so on. It only becomes morally suspect when it involves a deficient stance toward others. Some closely knit couples do indeed take such a stance, but by no means all close friendships involve such attitudes. If and when they do, it is appropriate for the school to condemn the attitudes and take steps to change them, rather than intervene prematurely and cast a suspicious eye on a morally praiseworthy situation.

It would be interesting to know more about teachers' attitudes toward close friendships between students. Is there any evidence, for instance, that there is a widespread wariness about friendship among teachers? If there is, why might this be? Do teachers feel in some way threatened by these relationships? Is it that some teachers have a moral outlook which gives a major place to moral rights and duties and in which there is no prominent place for a value like friendship? If so, perhaps that also explains why some teachers say they feel guilty about the time they spend helping children to cope with the problems their friendships are causing them.

Sometimes it is not the friendship itself that teachers take exception to, but the activities it involves. Respecting friendship and taking it seriously may mean that teachers will have to revise their views about gossip. It is commonplace for teachers to cast severe glances at gossiping girls (girls seem to attract this attention more than boys), even if the gossiping is happening in a break. But is this necessarily a morally reprehensible activity? That question needs a chapter in itself, not least to clarify the notion of gossip, but here let me just suggest that there are reasons for thinking that adolescent gossiping is not automatically to be condemned. There may be moral value in it. Sabini and Silver (1982), who define gossip as "idle evaluative talk about someone behind his back" (p. 92), see it as "a training ground for both self-clarification and public moral action" (p. 106). And Sissela Bok (1984), who deals in some detail with the harmful aspects of gossip, which she defines as "informal personal communication about other people who are absent or treated as absent" (Bok, 1984, p. 91), suggests that to condemn gossip absolutely is to

> fail to consider its extraordinary variety . . . [to] ignore the attention it can bring to human complexity, and [to be] unaware of its role in conveying information without which neither groups nor societies could function. (p. 101)

For adolescents, particularly, gossip may have an important role to play in the process of developing more finely differentiated moral attitudes toward the actions and attitudes of others.

It has been suggested that teachers might *show* the value of friendship in the everyday life of the school by being friends with their students. If we are talking here about friendliness, fine. The deeper, more intimate relationship, however, which has been the focus of this chapter, is, generally speaking, ruled out by the norms of impartiality that must govern the teacher's conduct. Just as doctors or lawyers would be likely to create ethical complexities for themselves if they entered into intimate personal relationships with their patients or clients, so it is with teachers. In the case of the teacher, there is the additional consideration of the immaturity of the students. So what does a teacher do if, in the middle of a math lesson, a tearful 6-year-old child raises a hand and says, "I haven't got any friends"? He responds, "But you have; I'm you're friend!" And when the child goes on to ask, "Will you play with me at recess, then?" he says, "Of course!" This real-life example illustrates superbly for me the kind of wisdom we expect, and usually get, as a matter of course from teachers. We expect that teachers will know just when in a clash of values one value must give way to another and know how to make the appropriate response in the context. This teacher was perfectly well aware of the demands of his professional role, but in this instance these demands had to give way to a response to a child who is feeling the misery of being friendless. A less perceptive teacher might have responded to the child's plea "Oh, I'm sure you have; I'm sure lots of people want to play with you" and then gone on with the math lesson. In so doing, he would have lost the chance to make a response that recognizes and underlines the value of friendship.[2]

So far the emphasis has been on restraint, on the need for the school not inadvertently to disvalue friendship in upholding other values. But

---

2. I am indebted to Cornel Hamm for this example.

is there anything the school can do *positively* to encourage friendship and the understanding of and valuing of friendship among students? One might perhaps first question whether it is appropriate for the school to do anything positive about friendship. Friendship, it might be claimed, is simply something that happens to one. Everyone, or almost everyone, comes across people they are particularly drawn to and, as a result, friendships develop and that's that. But, as Blum (1980) points out, friendships can exist at very different levels, and a relationship like the one between Kate and Sue has over time involved considerable effort on both their parts in overcoming obstacles to their deep commitment and care for each other. Such caring, far from being a natural process, is hard to achieve, and it may well be something that the school can help young people to understand and appreciate.

Let me, then, tentatively offer some suggestions about what the school might do *positively* about friendship.

In general, active efforts by the teacher to promote friendship among students will rightly be seen by them as officious meddling and will do more harm than good. Teachers of very young children, however, who are concerned to encourage friendship among their students along the lines that I have suggested parents might do, may from time to time discover this means that they have to take an active role. They may sometimes have to remind children of the obligations of friendship, help friends to resolve their disputes, and console a child who has been abandoned by his or her friend.

With adolescents, the teacher will be concerned not with the promotion of friendship, which would almost inevitably involve an unjustifiable interference in the lives of her students, but with deepening the understanding of the complexities of the phenomenon of human friendship. The teacher can help them to explore what it is to enter into a relationship in which both partners are deeply committed to each other. She can consider the downside of friendship in its various aspects—the conflicts that may exist with other values and those relationships that hinder the flourishing of one or both partners or, in the worst cases, destroy them. Here literature and film may well have an important role to play. Sometimes this may be incidental to the study of, say, a novel as part of the literature syllabus. Sometimes the teacher may deem it appropriate to focus explicitly on questions like those raised by the friendship between the determined Emma and the biddable Harriet in Jane Austen's *Emma*.

This last point raises the question of how desirable it is to encourage young people to become self-conscious about their own friendships in particular. To take a fairly familiar phenomenon, it may be important to young people in some contexts simply to be seen as having a friend, that is, not to be seen as friendless. And anyone who can reasonably respectably fill the role of friend is better than no one at all. Here friendship is clearly serving a purpose beyond itself, but it is one whose object, unlike that of the usual advantage friendship, involves the notion of friendship itself. Sometimes a relationship like this will persist for a while with few of the usual characteristics of a friendship simply because both parties want to preserve the picture of themselves as a person who has a friend. How wise is it for teachers to draw attention to this?

Most of the great classical treatises on friendship—those by Aristotle, Cicero, and Montaigne, for instance—do not allow for the possibility of friendship between women or between men and women. Had the authors not held views about the inferiority of women, it seems to me, they could have applied what they have to say about friendship without difficulty to those cases as well. Today, too, different views exist on the capacities of men and women for friendship. Discussion of views of alleged gender differences in this area also needs to find a place in education.

CONCLUSION

Dispositions like self-respect, self-esteem, and courage are clearly needed to sustain a democratic community. The fraternal feelings not focused on here that citizens should have toward fellow citizens are also, perhaps more obviously, linked to the democratic community. But the intimate notion of friendship that has been the focus of this chapter seems to me just as much to characterize a democratic society. In such a society friendship can be *publicly* celebrated as something of intrinsic value that may on occasion override other values. This would be an impossible public stance in a totalitarian society. In the latter, when friendship competes with the subject's allegiance to the party or state, it can never win out. The depiction of Jung Chang's (1993) father, in *Wild Swans*, perfectly exemplifies this absolutist position. For this man, communist principles and adherence to their interpretation by Chairman Mao always took precedence over his undoubted love for his wife and family. In this respect, in Mao's China, he was doing no more than a good citizen should. By contrast, democratic societies can tolerate the fact that sometimes people, exercising their moral judgment and not without misgivings and regret, will put the values of friendship above their political obligations. Perhaps this is the hallmark of democracy.

CHAPTER 6

Trust

Philosophical reflection (Baier, 1986; Bok, 1978; Luhmann, 1979) agrees with commonsense observation on the pervasiveness of trust in human life. Courage, friendship, self-respect, honesty—all unsurprisingly involve trust, since it is the bedrock underlying all imaginable forms of human life. But trust and, at appropriate times and places, distrust have, as I shall argue, a very particular role to play in democratic societies.

In complex societies two forms of trust are widespread. There is trust in institutions, for instance, money and the political process, as well as personal trust between individuals, for instance, friends, lovers, and colleagues. And as well as trust, there is also distrust. These facts raise a number of questions: What is trust? How is it, for instance, connected to seemingly related notions like expectation and hope? How, if at all, are trust in institutions and personal trust connected? Is it possible to distinguish between rational and pathological forms of trust, of both institutions and persons? How might trust of institutions and persons be created and maintained in a democratic, pluralist, multicultural society? Is distrust always to be seen negatively? Is there, for instance, a positive role for distrust in relation to institutions? What is the role of education in promoting trust (and perhaps distrust) in institutions? Can education make people trustworthy and also able rationally to assess when they should trust others?

This is a formidable list of questions. Writers in this field tend to discuss either trust in institutions from the point of view of economic/political theory *or* personal trust, but not both, and they certainly do not take on the issues raised for education as well. I need, however, to attempt the triathlon. Trust and distrust in institutions and people are learned. The school provides opportunities, whether or not its staff and students are aware of this, for learning attitudes of trust and distrust toward the institution of the school community, the wider political society, and perhaps groups within that society. In addition, members learn to trust (or distrust) one another on a personal level. The school may even be influential in shaping some of its students into basically trusting or basically distrustful, suspicious characters or people who see themselves as untrustworthy. These processes are all going on in the same institution, cutting across one another and perhaps cutting across attitudes that parents are encouraging or discouraging. It is necessary to achieve some understanding of these processes and to see how trust, and perhaps distrust, might be actively fostered to promote a flourishing democratic, multicultural society.

WHAT IS TRUST?

As Annette Baier (1986) has noted, despite the pervasive nature of trust in human life, there have been relatively few discussions of it in either classical or contemporary philosophical texts. Plato presumably expected the citizens of *The Republic* to trust the philosopher kings; Aristotle implicitly recognized the importance of trust in his discussion of friendship; John Locke gave a central role to trust in his discussion of legitimate government. This seems to be more or less the limit of classical treatments. Recently, however, social scientists and some political theorists have begun to consider trust, particularly in the context of cooperation. At the start of his monograph on trust, Niklas Luhmann (1979) refers to trust "in the broadest sense" as "confidence in one's expectations" (p. 4). Diego Gambetta (1988) summarizes the definition of trust shared by most of the papers in his edited book on trust and cooperation as follows:

> Trust (or, symmetrically, distrust) is a particular level of the subjective probability with which an agent assesses that another agent or group of agents will perform a particular action, both *before* he can monitor such action (or independently of his capacity ever to be able to monitor it) *and* in a context in which it affects *his own* action. . . . When we say we trust someone or that someone is trustworthy, we implicitly mean that the probability that he will perform an action that is beneficial or at least not detrimental to us is high enough for us to consider engaging in some form of cooperation with him. (p. 217)

These definitions highlight trust as a form of reliance on other people that involves beliefs about the likelihood of their behaving or not behaving in certain ways. As such, they illuminate aspects of economic and political behavior (particularly influenced perhaps by the prisoners' dilemma problem of game theory) involving formal voluntary relationships. They fail, however, to capture the kinds of relationships between parents and children, friends and lovers that seem perhaps obvious examples of trust relationships. Here trust seems to involve reliance on others' goodwill toward one (Baier, 1986). What seems to be common to all the very different phenomena falling under the concept is that trust is a form of belief. It is a matter of believing that you can rely on X. What makes a case of trust more than a matter of simply believing that X will be the case (e.g., the person will perform the beneficial action, will show goodwill toward you) is the element of risk involved. One believes despite the uncertainty. Related to the degree of uncertainty involved, there is a continuum of consciousness of the trust relationship. The risk of one's belief that one can rely on someone (or something) proving to be ill founded may be so slight that it may not enter one's consciousness. For instance, when I get on the bus in the morning, *as a matter of fact* I trust in the driver's competence. I do not in the normal case get on the bus with my heart in my mouth, willing it to be the case that we shall all arrive in one piece. My behavior, as I settle down to read my newspaper, shows my trust in the driver. On the other hand, if I accept a lift in a car from a driver whom I know to be notoriously accident-prone, I shall be conscious of the fact that I am taking a risk and that, despite what I know, I have decided (on this occasion at least) to trust him. My behavior shows this in that I do accept the lift and it shows the degree of my trust as I nervously grip the seat, take furtive glances at the wing mirrors, and so on. If I have no choice but to take the lift, I may just hope for the best rather than trust.

There is also another continuum in trust relationships, a continuum of feeling or commitment. At the extreme end of the continuum in trusting someone, I will, for instance, rely absolutely on their goodwill. This will be for me a deep commitment. This will typically be the case with lovers and in longstanding relationships between friends, but it may also be the attitude of some people toward their political leaders or members of the royal family. Our reactions will be different in the event of a breakdown in relationships at different ends of what might be called the commitment continuum. If our expectations are not met in those cases where our commitment is slight, we shall be disappointed, but if our absolute reliance on another's goodwill is met with ill will or indifference, we shall feel let down or betrayed.

Trust, then, involves the belief that you can rely on someone (e.g., specifically, their beliefs, dispositions, motives, goodwill) or something (e.g., the efficiency of a piece of equipment) where there is a greater or lesser element of risk. One may or may not be conscious of the trust relationship, and it will involve varying degrees of personal commitment. Here I shall be mainly concerned with those cases of trust in which there is reliance on beliefs about others' goodwill toward one, although I shall make reference to other sorts of trust.

PERSONAL TRUST

Let me now try to give a more detailed picture of a trust relationship. This is, in the first instance, an account of personal trust. In the next section, we shall see how much trust in institutions is similar.

Trust in the sense of reliance on the goodwill of another person is an attitude that typically has no definite beginning but grows slowly and may not be verbally acknowledged. More than that, it may be that one is not aware of one's reliance on the goodwill of another or that the other person may not acknowledge this reliance. In other words, there can be implicit trust, unwanted trust, and trust of which the trusted is unaware.

Trust relationships can be easily destroyed and are not easily repaired. This was the case in the relationship between James Joyce and Nora Barnacle when Joyce returned from Trieste to Dublin in 1909. There a former friend, Vincent Cosgrave, told him that, during Joyce's courtship of Nora five years earlier, he was seeing Nora on the nights when Joyce wasn't. This turned out to be a false claim, made maliciously, but Joyce's letters from Dublin to Nora in Trieste, at the time when he believed it to be true, reveal the dramatic effect it had on his feelings for her and his view of their relationship, despite the five happy years he had spent with her (Ellmann, 1975) . As Luhmann (1979) says:

> One falsehood can entirely upset trust and, by their symbolic value, quite small mistakes and misrepresentations can unmask the "true character" of somebody or something, often with unrelenting rigour. (p. 28)

Those who have been lied to are likely to be resentful, disappointed, and suspicious. They look back on their past beliefs and actions in the light of the lies they have been told and realize that they were manipulated. They become aware, for instance, that they were unable to make choices according to the most adequate information they could have had. They feel wronged and are wary of new overtures (see Bok, 1978). Both Baier (1986) and Luhmann (1979) have sensitive treatments of the supporting attitudes that are needed to maintain and repair trust relationships. Between them they stress, for instance, self-confidence, tact, delicacy of discrimination in appreciating what one is trusted with, good judgment as to whom to trust with what, and a willingness to admit and forgive fault. All of these will be more easily learned and appropriately exercised in a social climate that is supportive of trust.

Can one be too trusting? Are there perhaps pathological versions of the trust relationship? In one sense, the answer seems to be that there clearly are. Those who trust blindly, in the face of evidence suggesting that the trusted person is indifferent to their good or even ill disposed toward it, are frequently criticized for leaving themselves open to manipulation. The wife who continues to believe her husband's stories about working late at the office to get important export orders off on time or sudden summonses to weekend meetings with his boss to discuss export policy, after the director has told her at the staff dinner about the closure of the export department, may be regarded as culpably gullible by her friends. Such trust will be seen as moral weakness that should be replaced by a more carefully monitored trust. Trust, if it is to be rational, it will be argued, should be based on good grounds for confidence in another's goodwill or at least the absence of good grounds for expecting that person's ill will or indifference. Yet from the wife's point of view, it may seem wrong even to *think* that her husband is untrustworthy. Being circumspect in the relationship to which she has committed herself would be destructive of that relationship.

Certainly vigilance in monitoring personal relationships can go too far. Luhmann (1979) paints a horrifyingly convincing picture of a way of life in which distrust has become a habit, a routine. The distrustful person regards members of his family and colleagues as potential enemies against whom he must muster an array of defenses to protect himself. He needs more information all the time, and at the same time he narrows down the information he feels confident he can rely on. Like Sam in Isaac Bashevis Singer's (1990) "A Peephole in the Gate," who, having been deceived by a number of women (and deceiving more himself), concludes:

> All my thoughts led in one direction: there is no love, there is no loyalty. Those with whom you are close will betray you even faster than total strangers. (p. 114)

At the same time, the distrustful person can hardly avoid his distrust being perceived, and someone who sees himself as the object of distrust will hardly be disposed to see the cause of this in himself. Rather, he will react negatively to the distrustful person. In this way, distrust feeds on itself and the dispositionally distrustful person is likely to be a very lonely person. As George Eliot noted, "What loneliness is more lonely than distrust?" Both personal relationships and communities need to be protected from the damaging effects of distrust. As I have indicated above, both Baier and Luhmann are extremely sensitive to the issues raised by the repair of trust relationships. Drawing on their work, I shall consider some strategies for the repair of trust in communities in the next section, and I shall take up these issues again more generally in the section on "Trust: The Role of the School."

TRUST IN INSTITUTIONS

No pluralist democracy could survive simply on the basis of personal trust relationships between individuals; it requires a basis of social trust. What I have in mind by social trust in the democratic context is the widespread belief among citizens that the whole system is functioning to promote the well-being of all its members. By analogy with personal trust, citizens in a democracy need to believe that the institutions within which they are living are informed by goodwill toward all members of the society. This is most obviously where one link with the cluster of values in the toleration family comes in. In pluralist, multicultural societies, whatever precise form toleration takes, trust is needed. For instance, whether a stand-off, live-and-let-live relationship prevails toward individuals and groups in a society who are committed to values different from one's own, or whether a more positive attitude of concern to promote their flourishing holds, widespread trust in the supporting institutional framework is needed. For instance, it seems to be a necessary condition for social trust that citizens do not regard their society as structurally unfair (Dunn, 1988). Concretely, they need to believe that the society's legal, economic, and political rules and procedures are fair and are being fairly applied. As a corollary, they need to believe that when the system breaks down for any reason, there will be procedures and the political will for swift redress of any wrong. This is not to say that they have to believe that each and every official has the public good and the good of individuals at heart, although it is to be hoped that most will. They simply have to believe that the system as a whole works in such a way as to promote the good of its members. It is in fact a plus if this can be achieved despite the fact that some of its officials are motivated, for instance, by the thought of the monthly paycheck rather than the public good.

More broadly, as well as a belief in fairness and other democratic values, citizens need to have a more general attitude if trust is to be widespread. This is what, following Bernard Williams (1985), I earlier called social confidence (see Chapter 2). For a society to have social confidence is for its members to be conscious of its major values (though not necessarily self-conscious about them), to think them important (though not necessarily to think *about* them all the time), and to mutually reinforce them implicitly and sometimes explicitly. Social confidence and social trust are mutually supportive social values.

Social trust is at its best and strongest when nobody notices it. If it becomes a matter for public debate, it is because it is in need of repair. Widespread social trust has an invigorating effect on social and institutional life. Within institutions, for instance, it makes all kinds of initiatives possible. In a climate of trust, people will be prepared to try new patterns of working, make suggestions for changes, and so on because they know that, even if things do not turn out as anticipated, their colleagues will appreciate that they were acting in a spirit of goodwill.

How, then, is such social trust achieved? Certainly not by demands for it. The politician in a democracy who says "Trust me!" ought to be regarded with deep suspicion. In the late twentieth century we are only too aware of the dangers of investing a quasi-personal trust in political leaders, even elected representatives. A childlike trust in powerful political leaders and the systems over which they preside has too often proved disastrous.

How, then, to achieve an appropriate level, and kind, of social trust in democratic institutions? Luhmann (1979) reminds us of an illuminating answer in the light of the best practice in democratic systems. As he puts it: "The trust in systems as a whole can . . . depend decisively on trust being curtailed at critical points and distrust being switched in" (p. 92).

As others besides Luhmann have noted (Dunn, 1988; Shklar, 1984), a political system that wants to promote the well-being of all its citizens must have well-designed institutions into which distrust as a protective device has been built. An established democracy, for instance, will have a legal opposition, an independent judiciary, independent commissions of inquiry into matters of public concern, a free press, and, it is to be hoped, a vigilant public who will judge the government by what it does rather than by its rhetoric. These different bodies and devices will question how much government policies really do promote the well-being of individuals, groups, and/or the general public. They will do this by operating with two sorts of distrust that can be directed at persons or systems. First, there will be what might be termed fundamental distrust, which questions the goodwill of the person or, in the case of a system, the fundamental aims or ends of the system. Second, there will be procedural distrust, which is directed not at the person's goodwill but at her competence or personal qualities, or, in the case of a system, not at its aims but at its means or procedures. In this need for a fine balance between trust and distrust, institutional trust differs sharply from personal trust. In personal trust relationships, trust feeds on trust and when even hints of distrust creep in they tend to be destructive. A friendship is not enhanced by slight elements of distrust!

The place of distrust in institutions, however, is not altogether unproblematic, for distrust, particularly fundamental distrust, is a powerful destructive force. A system may be able to tolerate large amounts of procedural distrust as long as there is little fundamental distrust. As Luhmann (1979) points out, those social systems that require, or cannot avoid, distrusting behavior among their members must also have ways of preventing distrust from gaining the upper hand. For unless distrust is strictly controlled, it may become dangerously rampant and come into conflict with other important institutional values. A common way of "neutralizing" actions that indicate distrust is by explaining that they do not stem from a *true* distrust of the person at whom they are directed but are rather required by the role. This allows for distrustful actions while at the same time preserving the general ethos of trust between participants in the enterprise. An assistant in a local shop who demands identification before accepting a check from a regular customer will explain apologetically that, although she knows it's all right, the system demands this. The assistant is making it plain that there is no question of fundamental distrust or even procedural distrust of this customer. Attempts to safeguard institutional trust in this and similar ways may, of course, not work. The disclaimer may not be accepted. Indeed, it may not be a gracious disclaimer. Women, members of some ethnic groups, adolescents, and elderly people in our society may so regularly meet with distrust-disclaimers of various sorts ("We *always* ask for the spouse's occupation for credit for men or women"; "We *always* ask for a deposit"; "We *always* ask for driver identification") that they correctly see that they are regarded as belonging to a group to be treated with procedural distrust and perhaps even with fundamental distrust. In this way, the relationship between trust and distrust in institutions and the control of distrust itself relies on trust. The mechanisms of distrust—the supervision and the monitoring of government and other institutions—and the ways of controlling them themselves have to be trusted.

Trust, then, is the foundation of our most intimate personal relationships as well as of our social life. It is often called a device for dealing with the freedom of others (Dunn, 1988; Luhmann, 1979) in the absence of which we are simply left with hope. Trust, though, is no easy option. It is, in Luhmann's (1979) words, always "a gamble, a risky investment" (p. 24). Perhaps, however, it is a gamble always worth taking—for societies and for individuals. Alternatively, we have to contemplate a society in which treachery, betrayal, and dishonesty are rife and a suspicious, distrustful stance to the world is an individual's most rational attitude. As Diego Gambetta (1988) puts it:

If we are not prepared to bank on trust, then the alternatives in many cases will be so drastic, painful and possibly immoral that they can never be lightly entertained. (p. 235)

Even if we are persuaded, though, that we should take a gamble on trust, how do we go about laying our bets? How can institutional and personal trust be promoted? In the following section, I shall attempt to provide a few tentative answers to that question which start from the assumption that trust has to be learned.

TRUST: THE ROLE OF THE SCHOOL

Children will have been in trust relationships with those who are caring for them (see Spiecker, 1990), in a society in which there is *some* degree of social trust, before they ever enter a formal educational institution. The tasks of the school, crucially important ones in a pluralist, multicultural society, are to (1) instantiate social trust in its own ethos; (2) attempt to give its students an understanding of social trust and distrust in a democratic society; (3) encourage students to apply that understanding not only to their society but to the school as an institution; and (4) foster and maintain conditions for the development of personal trust between its members, as well as giving them an understanding of trust in personal relationships. All educational institutions, whether nursery schools or colleges, will be concerned to create conditions for personal and social trust, while the understanding of trust and the application of that understanding to the wider society and in the school situation will assume increasing importance in the later stages of education. This is no easy program for a school, which will have to be extremely careful that distrust does not get destructively out of hand.

Social Trust and School Ethos

Let us look first at social trust in the context of the ethos of the school. The school's contribution here is unique in the early years, since it is the institution where the child first encounters social trust (and distrust) as a participant in an institution. The first task of the school will be to *show* trust, sometimes, but not as a general rule, making this explicit. Its procedures, as far as possible, will be framed in such a way that, in and of themselves, they say: We trust you, that is, we confidently rely on your goodwill toward this community. British primary schools are often particularly good at this, giving individual children and groups of children responsibility for the conduct of many aspects of their school life—so much so that when they go on to the secondary school, where they are treated as "the babies" who need considerable supervision, children often feel resentful, since it seems to them that in this new institution they are not trusted.

In the nature of the case much of the attention that the school pays to the fostering and maintenance of social trust will be focused on the avoidance of negative messages. The school will want to avoid unwittingly conveying the impression to its students: We don't trust you or, even worse, some of you. The issues that arise here will present teachers with some dilemmas. On the one hand, as we have seen, in order to be trustworthy, any institution has to build into its procedures mechanisms of distrust, in the school case, for instance, procedures for checking on students' attendance. The significance of these may be misperceived by students. On the other hand, the school is concerned with other educational aims besides the creation and maintenance of trust, for instance, the promotion of knowledge and understanding, and the means it may employ in the realization of these aims may suggest that it does not trust its students. Teachers may judge, for instance, that the promotion of knowledge and understanding requires, among other things, the monitoring and supervision of young students' learning, and thus may ask parents to countersign homework. As a consequence, students may feel they are not trusted. This must present teachers with a problem, particularly if the countersigning of homework seems to be raising standards in academic work in the school.

It may be the case that the school's demonstration of lack of trust is not unwitting. School staff may believe that they have good grounds for not trusting some of their students. It is important, though, to say at this point that these will be *individuals* whom school staff believe bear the school ill will. Staff could not have good grounds for a blanket distrust of whole groups of students, say, those from a minority group. (How could they know that each individual bears the school ill will? If they do know this, then this would be to distrust them as individuals.) Students who feel themselves to be distrusted *as members of a group* can rightly object that they are victims of prejudice.

It is perhaps helpful to categorize the students whom a school staff will typically distrust as "criminals," "terrorists," and "outsiders." The criminals are those students who by and large accept the school's values and rules but who nevertheless persistently infringe them. These are the children who are always suffering the school's standard punishments. The terrorists are those students, few in most schools, who accept neither the school's values nor those of the wider society and will frequently attack the fabric of the school as well as other members of it. Finally there are the outsiders: students, perhaps coming from minority groups, who do not accept the school's major values and ethos. The extent of their commitment to the school, for instance, may be as a place to get necessary examination qualifications. They cause no problems, but to a large extent they live by values and have attitudes quite different from those that the school exemplifies in its ethos. Teachers must distrust the terrorists and show that they do so, because this is part of what it is to behave with social confidence in the school's ethos. In certain circumstances teachers will have good grounds for having (what will usually be a procedural) distrust of the criminals, although it is important that there be routes by which they (and indeed the terrorists, too, if that is possible) can regain trust, as I shall indicate in a moment. It is not clear, though, that school staff should regard the outsiders with suspicion, as they sometimes do. Here it seems that intolerance leads to a damaging attitude of fundamental distrust, which can only feed on itself. More appropriate here would be an attempt at dialogue to achieve some understanding of the values of the outsiders so that their flourishing can be a genuine aim of the school in a pluralistic democracy.

As far as distrusted individuals are concerned, however, ways have to be found for them to become trusted again. Circumstances will indicate different possibilities. It may be important to stress to the child and her peers that one or two lapses do not make someone an untrustworthy individual. Part of becoming a trustworthy person is seeing oneself as a person who can be trusted, not as some inherently leaky vessel. If Luhmann (1979) is right on the significance of punishment, penance, and pardon, it may be important for schools, particularly in the case of young children, to consider semiformal ways in which students might rehabilitate themselves in the eyes of other members of the community. These can have the function of indicating that the affair is closed and there is no further legitimate occasion for distrust.

This chapter cannot provide substantive solutions to these problems. What I hope it suggests is that teachers need to have some understanding of the issues raised by the notion of social trust in an educational institution if they are to approach the practical problems confronting them daily with insight and sensitivity. Understanding of these issues by individual teachers, however, is not sufficient. It must be complemented, as in the related case of social confidence (see Chapter 2), by the school's use of its resources *as an institution* to promote trust (and keep distrust within bounds). The school staff as a whole, not only teachers but support staff as well, need to discuss and frame together whole-school policies that instantiate democratic values and create and foster, rather than violate, social trust. At some point school governors, parents, and, where appropriate, students need to be involved in this process. The point of the deliberations will be the framing of policies that are supportive of a social ethos in which trust can for the most part be taken for granted and in which the conflicts and tensions highlighted above can, as far as possible, be resolved or at least recognized for what they are.

Understanding Social Trust and Distrust in a Democratic Society

In a pluralist society where trust may be under threat, teachers and other members of the school's staff need, then, to have an understanding of social trust if they are to create, maintain, and perhaps repair an ethos of trust in the school. What about students? For them, coming to understand social trust and the role of distrust is part of their political education in a democratic system. Building on the basis of their years of firsthand experience as members of the school as an institution, their political education can give them, probably at some quite late stage in their school education, a reflective understanding of the role of trust and distrust in a democratic system. Let me indicate some possible themes in that political education. A principal focus will be the grounds for trust in a political system. Why trust democracy? According to what criteria does the citizen decide to trust this party or this politician? Are they different from those he might use in personal relationships or face-to-face encounters? What is the nature of trust in an unequal power relationship? Relevant here will be some discussion of the role of distrust in democratic systems, and one problem will be that of encouraging a healthy skepticism of politicians and their claims without tipping students over into an apathetic cynicism. What is probably important here is the encouragement of realistic expectations. Luhmann (1979) refers to psychological research which indicates that if the possibility of some disappointment is built into an expectation, if we meet with a particular case of disappointment then the expectation is felt to be confirmed overall ("Yes, there are some crooked cops, but most of the police are doing a good job"). It will be important, too, to encourage an appreciation of the different objects of trust and distrust and how they are interrelated in the political area. As well as judgments about a politician's goodwill, there are judgments to be made about his competence and in some cases about his motives. This is not the place to work out where, and in what precise form, in the schema of a political education a treatment of the roles of trust and distrust should occur. My intention has been only to indicate that there is a need for some understanding of these notions.

Application of Notions of Trust and Distrust to Society and School

An important, but delicate, area in education for social trust and distrust is that of the application of these notions to society and the school itself. Dangers abound here. Generally speaking, it is important for teachers to try to guard against the blinders that hamper us all. For, in encouraging distrust of *our* bogeymen, it is all too easy to nurture an implicit trust in things that need to be questioned. A friend of mine said that his parents and teachers effectively got him to distrust strange men who might offer him rides in cars but never so much as suggested that he might extend the same wariness to the government. Is the counsel of perfection perhaps to try to encourage students at least to entertain a distrust of one's idols? If so, this has to be managed in a way that does not take a nihilistic turn, leaving students feeling that there is nothing worth valuing.

More particularly, in a democratic society it will be right for students to entertain and, where appropriate, express distrust of the school as an institution. For, as I have argued above, such distrust is democracy's chief protective device, and there is no reason to exempt the school from its searchlight. If, however, there is not only massive procedural but also fundamental distrust, this will be totally destructive of the school's efforts in all areas of its life. As a model of a responsive democratic institution, therefore, the school should be quick to pick up on the first signs of distrust. Concretely, this will mean having an openness to students' views in both formal and informal ways and being prepared seriously to consider those views. This will be possible in a school with a strong ethos of social trust, as outlined above.

Fostering Personal Trust Among Students

What can the school do about fostering personal trust relationships among its students? Even more so than in the case of social trust, the role of the school cannot be an aggressively positive one—it cannot demand that its students trust each other—but it can provide invaluable support for such relationships. It can create space for them, and sensitive teachers can nurture them and help their students when they are faced with the downside of trust relationships—distrust, suspicion, and betrayal. In this respect the school should play the same supporting role in relation to trust relationships as it should in the closely related (indeed overlapping, since trust is centrally involved in friendship) matter of friendships between students discussed in the previous chapter.

Perhaps most importantly in a pluralist, multicultural society like our own, the common school provides a meeting ground in which people from different groups can form personal relationships in an environment relatively protected from the extremes of prejudice. (This, in my view, is one powerful argument against separate schools for different ethnic or religious groups.) For the growth of trust in personal relationships is a slow, tentative business in which each party cautiously tests the ground. It is likely to be most successful when both parties are relatively self-confident, so that they are not daunted by small setbacks and can both acknowledge and forgive faults. A sensitive teacher can be immensely helpful in this process by being aware of the pitfalls in forming and maintaining trust relationships and unobtrusively encouraging a student to have more realistic expectations, to take a more tactful approach, to appreciate what she is being trusted with, and to be prepared to see a betrayal, now bitterly regretted, for the single mistake that it was. Teachers, especially teachers of young children, often spend a great deal of time helping children to form relationships with other children, supporting them when the relationships are foundering or helping them to repair and reestablish them. Some, it seems, feel guilty about the time they spend in this way, but they should surely not do so in the light of the fundamental importance of these relationships.

Unlike the understanding of social trust, the promotion of students' understanding of trust in personal relationships is likely to be most helpfully pursued in an informal way. Could there be any point in formal talks on aspects of the nature of trust, except perhaps for budding philosophy students? It will occur in the process of coming to understand and appreciate many books and films—*Othello* is only one obvious example—and on those occasions when the teacher is attempting to help students with problems of conflicts of loyalties and betrayal. For these latter occasions are not to be seen simply as a matter of the teacher appearing like a helpful automobile repair person, but as occasions when students sometimes achieve acute insights into personal relationships of lasting significance for them.

CHAPTER 7

Honesty

Encouraging children to be honest looks like one of the more straightforward of the teacher's tasks. Indeed, teaching children that it is wrong to lie, steal, cheat, and make promises they do not mean to keep is something that it is taken for granted teachers will do as they teach reading, geography, algebra, or whatever. Even the Hillgate Group (Cox et al., 1986), which thinks that the school should be first and foremost a place where children acquire academic disciplines, lists honesty among the five values that it thinks the school must inculcate. The group does not elaborate further on what might be involved, so perhaps its members assume that encouraging children to be honest is something that teachers, as morally mature people, can take in their stride without reflecting on what it involves. I want to suggest that even in the supposedly "straightforward" cases, that is not so. Furthermore, to give children a sensitive understanding of this area of the ethical life requires considerable thought and exploration by teachers, both individually and collectively. And without it, an education in democratic citizenship is incomplete.

THE STRAIGHTFORWARD CASES: STEALING AND LYING

So, what problems do the straightforward cases of lying, stealing, cheating, and making false promises raise for the teacher? First, they are not all of a piece. Stealing is a matter of wrongfully appropriating property to which one has no right. Lying, cheating, and making false promises might be roughly characterized as a matter of intentionally giving a false picture of the way you believe things to be. Honesty, then, has at least two aspects—uprightness in matters of property and veracity, which is a virtue of speakers. This distinction is a fairly rough-and-ready one, and one can think of cases falling under the veracity aspect that might be said to deprive someone of something which is rightfully theirs. Slander and libel might be said to deprive someone of (the property of) their good reputation. Perhaps a problematic one for the teacher is cheating, copying someone else's work and presenting it as one's own. How is one to present the wrongness of cheating to the child? Is it that the child who cheats is giving the teacher, her classmates, and her parents a false picture of her knowledge, skills, and so on; or is she to be seen as getting through deceit something she does not deserve—marks, recognition, perhaps praise from the teacher? In school, as a matter of fact, it is usually the former aspect that is stressed. Attention is focused on the harm the child is doing to herself in giving those concerned with her education a false picture, with the result that their efforts cannot be as effective as they would be if they knew exactly what her problems were, what she does not understand, and so on. In other contexts, in the academic world, for instance, the focus is likely to be on the wrongness of getting something one does not deserve, recognition perhaps for ideas that one has plagiarized, which may sometimes involve depriving a colleague of his rightful recognition (sometimes complicated by the fact that the undeserved rewards may be in part financial). How much should teachers draw attention to the wrongness in cheating as the getting by stealth of what one does not deserve? To do this will involve entering into the complex area of issues of fairness to do with just deserts (see, e.g., Sher, 1989). Teaching children not to steal, even leaving aside the questions raised by the presentation of the wrongness of cheating, is a complex task. For simply to get children to understand why stealing is wrong will involve seeing that they have some understanding of the notion of property, the notion of rights on which that depends, and the possibility of institutions of both private property and common property. It will also involve encouraging children to examine how far these institutions are necessary in any human community. Having simply gestured at some of the complexities in the case of uprightness in matters of the property aspect of honesty, let me turn to the veracity aspect.

Is encouraging the virtue of veracity a matter of encouraging children always to speak the truth, to give an accurate picture of the way they believe things to be, "the whole truth and nothing but the truth"? Curiously perhaps, the answer is not an unqualified yes. Reflection on our talk will reveal that rather rarely are we expected to offer our hearers the complete, unvarnished truth. Certainly when we are trying not to bore people, not to impose our troubles on them, we do not offer the whole truth. Asked how we are doing, how our vacation was, we reply fine, great, rather than offer a catalogue of minor ailments or an exotic collection of travelers' tales. In fact, we have to learn that only in special contexts (for instance, in a police investigation or perhaps in the hunt for some bit of lost property) does our interlocutor really want the whole truth, every detail. Many anecdotes would gain nothing if related with strict regard for the whole truth. Flirting, after-dinner speeches, and cheering people up would be lackluster affairs if pursued with forensic attention to truth. Perhaps having a proper perspective on truth in these matters is being able to enjoy them even while thinking, "Well, he would say that, wouldn't he?" The honest person, then, does not have to tell the whole truth all the time; he has to know when it is appropriate to do so. As Annette Baier (1990) puts it:

> For veracity is knowing *when* one is bound to speak one's mind and then speaking it as best one can. Even then, fallible judgment will be involved, snap decisions concerning how most helpfully to speak it, what sentences to produce. (p. 270; emphasis in original.)

Children, too, have to learn to recognize when other people are, without being mendacious, not speaking the whole truth. Much of the teasing fun adults have with young children exploits the fact that, not being initiated into the complexities of social life, children tend to take everything seriously. Learning that someone can be only joking, just teasing, involves learning that social intercourse is not always a matter of the exchange of the whole truth.

Children will learn, then, when a strict account of what they believe to be the case, with no cutting of corners, is not to the point. In the interests of good manners and sociability, either judicious editing or fanciful embroidery is called for. They will also need to consider how they are to cope with the more difficult question of what to do in those cases where truth is very much to the point but where other considerations, perhaps of other people's, or their own, well-being, pull in the opposite direction. The classic case is that discussed by Kant of the lie to the murderer looking for his victim, which perhaps most people would hold to be justified by concern for the potential victim. If there is to be any case where honesty might be overridden by other considerations, this is surely it. Kant's (trans. 1949) claim, though, as is well known, is that even in this case to be honest "is a sacred and absolutely commanding decree of reason, limited by no expediency." It is interesting, however, to look in detail at his reply to Benjamin Constant's attack on his views.

> For instance, if by telling a lie you have prevented murder, you have made yourself legally responsible for all the consequences; but if you have held rigorously to the truth, public justice can lay no hand on you, whatever the unforeseen consequences may be. After you have honestly answered the murderer's question as to whether this intended victim is at home, it may be that he has slipped out so that he does not come in the way of the murderer, and thus that murder may not be committed. But if you had lied and said he was not at home when he had really gone out without

your knowing it, and if the murderer had then met him as he went away and murdered him, you might justly be accused as the cause of his death. For if you had told the truth as far as you knew it, perhaps the murderer might have been apprehended by the neighbors while he searched the house and thus the deed might have been prevented. Therefore, whoever tells a lie, however well intentioned he might be, must answer for the consequences, however unforeseeable they were, and pay the penalty for them even in a civil tribunal. This is because truthfulness is a duty which must be regarded as the ground of all duties based on contract, and the laws of these duties would be rendered uncertain and useless if even the least exception to them were admitted. (quoted in Bok, 1978, p. 269)

Despite the last sentence of the quoted passage, which draws attention to the ultimate reason for telling the truth, Kant's main preoccupation here seems to be how, if we are unhappily in this situation confronted by the murderer seeking his victim, we avoid *legal blame*. This comes out in several places. If you stick rigidly to the truth, "public justice can lay no hand on you." If you tell a lie, you are responsible for the unforeseen consequences and may "justly be accused" and "pay the penalty for them even in a civil tribunal." Bernard Williams (1985) has drawn attention to the significance of blame in the "peculiar institution" of morality, and certainly here Kant seems to be suggesting that a very good reason for sticking to the rules (in this case, those of truth-telling) is that at least then we cannot be legally blamed for whatever goes wrong. After all, we "only told the truth." Is it always likely to be the case, though, that the course of action that is least likely to result in attracting legal blame to one is necessarily the wisest in a conflict-of-principles situation? If not, there seems to be something rather self-indulgent in making considerations about such blame universally central to one's deliberations in the matter of difficult ethical choices.

If, then, there is no compelling reason always to make truth trumps in any situation where we are faced with conflicting ethical considerations, the teacher's job is once again a difficult one. She doesn't have ready to hand out the neat rule "Always tell the truth." She has to make her own professional judgments (as do doctors, nurses, journalists, etc.) about when considerations other than truth should be overriding, *and* she has to initiate her students into the complex world of conflicting considerations and fallible judgment in choosing between greater and lesser evils. For instance, is it best to keep silent on some occasions? Depending on the context, that may be dishonest, it may be weak or cowardly, or it may be the kindest or most prudent course of action.

The "straightforward" cases of lying and stealing require a much fuller treatment (see Bok, 1978, for an entire book on the first of these;

see also Michell, 1990, for a treatment of patriarchy's pressure on veracity), but the ethical complexities of honesty do not end there, as the next section indicates.

CANDOR

I have suggested that wariness about attracting legal blame seems to be prominent in Kant's discussion of one's obligation to tell the truth to the murderer seeking his victim. This same wariness leads Kant to a different conclusion in the matter of candor. In Kant's (trans. 1963) view, "No man in his true senses . . . is candid" (p. 224). Reserve and reticence are our protection against mockery and censure by our fellows. If we were wholly good, we would not need to be reserved, but as it is we are so full of defects that if we revealed these in a free and frank way we should become "foolish and hateful" in other people's eyes. We have, as Kant says, "to keep the shutters closed." If we are prudent we do not open our hearts even to intimate friends.

> We must so conduct ourselves towards a friend that there is no harm done if he should turn into an enemy. We must give him no handle against us. . . . It is very unwise to place ourselves in a friend's hands completely, to tell him all the secrets which might detract from our welfare if he became our enemy and spread them abroad. (Kant, trans. 1963, p. 208)

The passage continues with advice about the need for care because, even if our friends do not turn into enemies, they might inadvertently do us harm, particularly if they are hot-headed.

What, then, is candor? It is being open about one's thoughts and feelings as a part of one's character. A person could be appropriately honest in the straightforward cases discussed in the previous section but not be a candid person. Kant, if he followed his own precepts, was an honest man but certainly not one to open his heart, not even to his friends. Chris, in Julian Barnes's (1981) *Metroland*, tells us that he was pushed into candor by his French girlfriend, Annick. After he has found it hard to tell her that he felt a mixture of "gratitude and smugness" after she first spent the night with him, he asks her how she felt:

> "I felt amused, at sleeping with an Englishman, and relieved that you could speak French, and guilty about what my mother would say, and eager to tell my friends what had happened, and . . . interested."
>   I then made some stumbling, embarrassed remarks in praise of her sincerity, and asked her how she had taught herself to act as she did. "What

do you mean, taught? It's not something you learn. Either you say what you mean or you don't. That's all."

That sounded rather less than all at first; but gradually I understood. The key to Annick's candor was that there was no key. (pp. 100–101)

The context of Chris's propulsion into candor is not surprising because, as Mark Fisher (1990) says, "love conduces to openness and guardedness diminishes love" (p. 31, n. 9). Pace Kant, it is characteristically in relationships between lovers and intimate friends that one finds such openness. One of the goods of such relationships is the possibilities they afford for people to be themselves and to enjoy discovering the unique combination of dispositions, thoughts, and feelings that make the other person the person she is. (This is not to say that such relationships will always be characterized by total candor, not least because concern for people we love may sometimes lead us to shield them from what seem to us unpalatable truths.) Candor is not only displayed in such intimate relationships, however; it is an attitude that can be apparent in all a person's dealings with other people. It is the attitude, I think, that Aristotle has in mind when he describes "the truthful man" as not "the man who keeps faith in his agreements, i.e. in the things that pertain to justice or injustice (for this would belong to another excellence), but the man who in the matters in which nothing of this sort is at stake is true both in word and in life because his character is such" (*Nicomachean Ethics*, 1127b 1).

Can candor be taught? Perhaps Annick was right about this. It certainly does not seem to be something to be taught as one might try to teach children that they should keep their promises and respect others' property. It seems rather to be a quality about which the teacher needs to nurture understanding in young people so that they see what kind of life is and is not compatible with it. This will in part involve dispelling some false conceptions of candor. It is to be equated neither with brutal frankness, telling people "home truths," nor with simple loquaciousness. It will also involve showing that with candor, as with other things, there is something like an Aristotelian mean. Letting it all hang out, even in the case of the most engaging people, may be less than enthralling for one's listeners if they are treated too regularly or at too great length to one's disclosures. One's candid revelations may lead in some cases to unwelcome intrusions into others' privacy. Also, there is something to be said for Kant's caution in that reasonable prudence will sometimes require that people be circumspect in revealing their thoughts and feelings. Perhaps, for instance, many perfectly amicable professional relationships would not benefit if colleagues revealed their thoughts and feelings on politics, religion, or diverse other subjects. This is the very stuff of novels in which we, as readers, are privy to the narrator's thoughts—thoughts that, if revealed to other characters, would cause them distress or to feel some unwanted emotion (pity, contempt) toward the narrator. That having been said, more positively, the teacher can present candor as an attractive quality. Candid people are likely to be well-intentioned people, as Baier (1990) says:

> It may . . . take a certain sweetness, trust and innocence of temper to be willing to open one's mind freely to others, so that the person with aggressive intentions will sensibly avoid candor. (p. 274)

Candid people (well-intentioned people with judgment about when, and to what degree, openness about thoughts and feelings is appropriate) are liked because we feel we know where we are with them, we feel at ease (as Chris says in *Metroland*, "Annick was the first person with whom I truly relaxed"), and they offer us an intimate picture of another perspective on the world. In addition to promoting an understanding of candor, the school, even if it cannot make people candid, can try to ensure that it has the kind of organization and atmosphere in which candor can flourish. To see what this might involve, it is useful to examine the reasons people fail to be candid.

OBSTACLES TO HONESTY AND CANDOR

Sometimes habitually honest people will tell lies or be less than candid in the interest of their own, or others', well-being; and unless one takes the view that honesty is a principle that should never be overridden, in many cases this will be the best thing to do.

The situation that bears a closer inspection, however, is that of the community which makes it very difficult for people to be, generally speaking, honest and candid. Some belief systems, for instance, may give people a powerful motive for hypocrisy, encouraging them either to hide beliefs and feelings they have been told are wrong or to pretend to noble and disinterested intentions they do not have. Characteristically, these are systems, like the Puritan version of Christianity or some extreme versions of Marxism, that expect people to live up to impossibly high ideals. Setting oneself up as holier-than-thou or as the all-Soviet man is a common enough reaction to such systems to have been a frequent target for lampoons. For the possibility of hypocrisy creates the anti-hypocrite. The result is a rather horrible society in which people are driven by impossible demands (for instance, for purity in thought, word, and deed), fearful of not fulfilling them, and at the same time suspicious of their neighbors, who surely cannot be all they seem. We are all too familiar with the resulting witch hunts—colleagues informing on colleagues, children informing on their parents. But it is worth pausing to ask how this vicious circle in the pursuit of purity gets started. The problem seems to be that the fierce exigency of the demands made on people fuels the hypocrisy/antihypocrisy circle. Such systems have no place for the idea that it is only human to make mistakes.

These examples of systems that might be said to encourage dishonesty and discourage candor are not simply of historical interest. For schools can set themselves up as systems that expect too much of their staff and students. In the past, schools did this, for instance, in expecting all children to keep up with the fastest learners in the class (copying someone else's work was one way of doing this) or to produce neatly written work in ink the first time without mistakes. (One of my youthful crimes was illicitly to remove pages from my English exercise book because I could not do this.) It is tempting to think that we have come a long way since those days and that we have a more reasonable attitude toward those things. And, indeed, we may have come a long way on these issues. However, we make our own impossible demands that fail to recognize human frailty. Schools will, for instance, rightly have antiracist and antisexist policies. These will recognize that the societies in which we currently live have been shaped along racist and sexist lines and that we need to redraw the groundplan, and to this end much constructive work is done in schools. For some antisexist and antiracist Puritans, however, it is not enough that people recognize the problems, struggle to reorient themselves, adapt to new manners, and help to build new institutional structures. They expect a world of New Men and Women, pure in thought, word, and deed, as of now. Much energy is then spent in attempting to identify the unregenerate racist or sexist behind the "hypocritical facade." But do we want to lock ourselves into the pursuit of purity in this way? For a start, why do we have to talk about a facade? We might just as easily welcome the fact that, for instance, some men recognize that in some public contexts certain kinds of behavior that are patronizing to women are no longer acceptable. We also do not have to emphasize the picture of the true (racist and sexist) inner self waiting to be exposed behind the public facade; rather we might highlight the more hopeful image of people who have been willing to change their behavior in one context perhaps being prepared, over time, to examine their attitudes and behavior in other contexts.

Schools can discourage candor not only by imposing high ideals from which any falling short must be punished but also by offering too limited a picture of the possibilities for human flourishing. Many schools in Britain, for instance, have come to see that, often unwittingly, their teaching, the organization of the school, letters to parents, and so on assume that the world is composed of heterosexual people, most of them couples bonded together in nuclear families. If children, especially younger children, get the idea that there is a normal family situation that their own does not fit, they may be anxious to conceal it in case they are ridiculed by fellow students or in some way might bring contempt on themselves or their families.

If a school wants to encourage candor, it needs not only to be sensitive to human frailty and to have a generous attitude toward staff and students who fall short of the ideals it is fostering; in a pluralistic society, it needs also to be sensitive to the different possible values and related ways of life to which its students may be committed. This, of course, is not to say that in the interests of candor the school should welcome all lifestyles (those, for instance, involving drugs or violence) so that its students have nothing they need be secretive about. It is to suggest that the school needs to take care that it is not *inadvertently* causing its students to feel ashamed of some aspects of their lives and constrained to hide these. Finally, the school should not attempt to get its students to feel something like an obligation to candor. The object is rather to achieve an atmosphere in which people do not feel obliged to hide things but in which they can choose to keep things private (but see Houston, 1993, for a sensitive treatment of the risks and dangers involved in encouraging candor in school).

SELF-KNOWLEDGE AND SELF-DECEPTION

It is often assumed that any teacher should encourage her students to have as honest a picture as possible of their own abilities, skills, and potentialities. The bogey here is self-deception. While discussions of whether it is possible for a person to deceive herself are legion, the everyday phenomena captured by this dramatic term, however they are to be accounted for theoretically, are familiar to most people. It certainly seems possible for people to have beliefs about themselves—that they are not ambitious, not easily offended, could run an efficient business if they had the chance—that others may feel there are strong grounds for doubting. At first sight it might seem important that people being educated should have a clear view of their personal qualities and potentialities. But is this really what is important educationally? R. K. Elliott (1989) suggests that having too realistic a view of one's potentialities could inhibit many desirable ventures:

> Teachers do not always want their pupils to make realistic judgements about what they can or cannot do. . . . There are many occasions in education, as in ordinary life, where success depends more on audacity and keeping one's nerve than on realistic judgement. In adolescence, when students have chosen what they are to specialise in, commitment to a chosen subject often begins to show itself by the student's exhibiting signs of excessive confidence: he starts to write in a would-be sophisticated and pretentious manner, becomes peremptorily critical of the accepted authorities in his subject, tries to produce positive original ideas of his own, and perhaps rejects what he regards as the pedestrian opinions of his teacher. No doubt he is in a state of illusion, both concerning his present ability and his potentiality, yet the development is of a type that will give the teacher more satisfaction than it causes him anxiety. The student is not so much pretending to be a critic (for example) as throwing himself into his project of becoming a critic: it is a serious pretence, if it is a pretence at all, since he intends to become the animal whose mask he is wearing; it is not an elaborate gesture to deceive. His exaggerated confidence reflects the energy he has invested in his venture, and helps him to make the desired transition successfully. Realistic judgement based on self-knowledge would be unlikely to serve him so well. If there is an element of self-deception in his attitude, even that is felt to be acceptable from a pedagogical point of view. (p. 52)

Teachers need, then, fine judgment about exactly when to get their students to take an unvarnished view of their abilities if they are to enable them to achieve all that they could. Ideally, they will need to consider this not only as individuals but also as a whole staff so that, even in the likely event that consensus is not achieved on all aspects of these difficult issues, at the least school policies can reflect an encouragement of risk-taking in intellectual and artistic pursuits. This perspective on self-deception may also perhaps require critical consideration of some of the self-assessment and profiling schemes popular in British schools, which require students realistically to assess their achievements and aspirations.

HONESTY AND POLITICAL EDUCATION

The discussion of honesty thus far has concentrated largely on its private aspects, but issues of honesty figure largely in public life. As Bernard Williams puts it:

It is a predictable and probable hazard of public life that there will be situations in which something morally disagreeable is clearly required. To refuse on moral grounds ever to do anything of that sort is more likely to mean that one cannot seriously pursue even the moral ends of politics. (p. 63)

One of the morally disagreeable things that may well be required is deceit in various guises. This is an aspect of political education that needs careful handling if students are not to become unjustifiably cynical about political matters. For a start, students will need to understand the nature of democratic adversarial politics, which demands the vigorous advance of policies, an ability to overlook the fact that a short while ago something quite different was being advocated, and a tendency to allow no value at all to one's opponents' views. This is not to suggest that there is nothing wrong with such a system, but it is not necessarily as dishonest as it might appear at first sight. It is important for students to see it for what it is and not as a wholly dishonest business where lies and distortions are simply traded between the different parties. They need, too, to be able to distinguish between cynical untruths told so that parties get reelected and, for instance, denials of impending devaluation to prevent unfair profits to speculators. The treatment of honesty in political life and in other aspects of public life (for instance, the law, medicine, and the media) as part of the political education the school offers needs considerable further discussion. Here I can do little more than point out that the school has two opportunities to politically educate its students about these matters: through the formal curriculum and through its own structures and ethos. The latter may well be the more powerful influence, and, for this reason alone, again the whole school staff needs to be involved in a review of its procedures from the point of view of their honesty and openness. British schools have been notoriously prone to secrecy. It was not uncommon, for instance, a few years ago for schools (typically schools for young children) standardly to have notices at the entrance forbidding parents to cross the threshold. Any school staff needs to take a critical look at their procedures to make sure that their practices fit their reflective beliefs about the kind of ethos they want to create.

CONCLUSION

In this chapter I have only looked at one element of the ethical world—teaching children to be honest in a number of its aspects—and there is more to be said about all of those. Further questions, not considered at all, spring to mind: Can one have trust in either personal relationships or institutions without honesty? How far is personal autonomy possible in a situation lacking in honesty and openness? If children are to be taught to be honest, won't they also have to be taught to be courageous, since sometimes one needs courage to be honest? If, as I have implicitly done, one rejects the Kantian justification for honesty, why in general is it a good thing to be honest? Is there a case for saying that rules about honesty should be more stringent in the public sphere? And as these questions indicate, helping children to acquire an understanding of honesty will involve a nuanced understanding of many other values, as well as trust and courage—values like friendship, love, and loyalty. Philosophers of education need to explore these complex and often tangled webs of values with teachers if they are to be adequate to the ethical demands of their profession. Teachers otherwise cannot do an honest job.

CHAPTER 8

Decency and Education
for Citizenship

Decency and good manners do not get much attention from those who write about democracy. Books and papers about citizenship or political education in a democracy stress the importance of fostering commitment to the principles underlying democracy—justice, freedom, respect for persons—and of the need for citizens to understand their duties, responsibilities, and rights and perhaps to have certain skills. Sometimes attention is drawn to the need for citizens to have qualities like courage, openmindedness, and so on. There is, however, no highlighting, usually, indeed, no mention, of decency or good manners.

And why should there be? Many people have not regarded the life of decency as self-evidently a good thing. Alexander Pope (Hayward, 1983) says in "Of the Characters of Women":

> She speaks, behaves, and acts just as she ought;
> But never, never reach'd one gen'rous Thought.
> Virtue she finds too painful an endeavour,
> Content to dwell in Decencies for ever. (p. 210)

This was echoed roughly two centuries later by Robert Lowell (1964):

> Terrible that old life of decency
> without unseemly intimacy
> or quarrels, when the unemancipated woman
> still had her Freudian papa and maids! (p. 86)

Even from its defenders, like Frances Hinton in Anita Brookner's *Look at Me*, praise for decency is hardly fulsome:

> I see no harm in the bourgeois way of life, myself. I like regularity of behavior and courtesy of manner and due attention paid to the existence of other people. I like an ordered life and discretion and reliability. And honesty. And a sense of honour. (Brookner, 1982, p. 59; quoted in Kekes, 1989, p. 71)

Many adolescents, too, find values like personal integrity, self-expression, and justice more powerfully appealing than the notion of decency.

I want to claim, however, that the values of decency are not simply an option for people who *happen* to like them, like Frances Hinton; they are essential ingredients of good lives in a democracy (as it is characterized earlier in this book and in White, 1983) because they make possible relationships with other members of one's society, who are not one's intimates, that are characterized by something like a mixture of goodwill, politeness, helpfulness, and forethought for others' needs and wants.

What exactly do I have in mind, then, in talking about the values of decency? In an attempt to answer that question, let me do two things. First, let me very concretely suggest ways in which societies and institutions marked by a spirit of decency differ from ones in which this is lacking, and let me also suggest what individuals lack who do not have decent manners. Then let me set out what I understand by the values of decency, and in particular democratic decency, and defend the latter against possible objections. This will make it possible to sketch the role of the school in promoting the values of decency as part of its education for citizenship in a democracy.

THE VALUES OF DECENCY

The presence or absence of the spirit of decency in a social situation is suggested by two contrasting experiences I had in 1989 in cafés in Warsaw and Vancouver. In Vancouver, the waitress smiled at me as I went in, helped me find a table, was happy to chat in a friendly way when taking my order, and throughout my meal was pleasantly attentive without being obsequious or embarrassingly fulsome. She apologized when an item on the menu was not available and suggested possible alternatives. I felt at ease and enjoyed my meal. In Warsaw, I was taken to a café in a park. Only one other table was occupied. A waiter leaned against the wall, viewing us idly but making no move to come over to us. Eventually he eased himself off the wall, sauntered over, and stood blank-faced by our table. The café had none of the things we asked him for—in fact, it had very little at all—and he had no alternative suggestions to offer. Eventually we ordered glasses of lemonade and drank them while the waiter stared sullenly at us. We felt awkward. My hosts were deeply embarrassed and lamented the rude, uncouth nature of their public life, which they saw as part of the legacy of more than 40 years of totalitarian rule. I offer these two incidents as two snapshots, one of a social situation characterized by decency and one in which it is lacking.

I am not concerned to praise or blame the protagonists or to explore possible extenuating circumstances in the second case. I simply want to show in a concrete way the kind of attitudes I have in mind. In a similar way, John Kekes vividly presents the difference between a society that embraces the values of decency from one which does not. He contrasts a description by Dennis Brogan of the atmosphere in a small town in Illinois, an atmosphere of "ease . . . general friendliness and candor," with a description which occurs in the correspondance of Boris Pasternak and Olga Friedenberg of a society characterized by "base, trivial hostility, unconscionable spite breeding petty intrigues" (quoted in Kekes, 1989, p. 51).

What is lacking in Kekes's second case, as it was in the Warsaw café, is decency: what Kekes describes as "a mixture of spontaneous goodwill, casual friendliness, a spirit of mutual helpfulness" (p. 51). It does not assume intimacy or involve deep feelings and thus can characterize the relationship between strangers or less-than-close colleagues in an enterprise. The attitudes and behaviors characteristic of decency tend to be mutually reinforcing; but if such attitudes are continually met with indifference or rudeness, then decency will not survive and there will be a slide into trivial hostility or worse.

At the individual level, Hume gives us further insight into the nature of good manners in a discussion of "Qualities Immediately Agreeable to Others." Hume sees good manners as, in part, the device whereby we attempt to control our pride and self-conceit and our great propensity to overvalue rather than undervalue ourselves. Good manners in conversation will mean, for instance, that

> Among well-bred people a mutual deference is affected; contempt of others disguised, authority concealed, attention given to each in his turn; an easy stream of conversation maintained, without vehemence, without interruption, without eagerness for victory, and without any airs of superiority. . . . In conversation the lively spirit of dialogue is agreeable, even to those who desire not to have any share in the discourse; hence the teller of long stories or the pompous declaimer is very little approved of. But most men desire likewise their turn in the conversation and regard with a very evil eye that loquacity which deprives them of a right they are naturally so jealous of. (Hume, ed. 1959, pp. 244–245)

The control of egoism and arrogance of all kinds is certainly in large part what decency and good manners are about. The person who does not feel and express gratitude, for instance, can be seen as trapped in an egoism that stands in the way of good manners. Such a person may either be selfishly preoccupied with the good she has received or implicitly feel that it is wholly appropriate that others should be ministering to her wants (see Casey, 1990, p. 156). But, as Hume's discussion brings out, the control of an overdeveloped sense of self-concern is only part of what decency is about. The other side of decency, perhaps its more gracious aspect, is concerned with making oneself agreeable or pleasing to others. Taking some care over how we dress, for instance, when invited out need not be a matter of vanity: It can be one of the ways in which we indicate that we are pleased by the invitation.

So far I have attempted, impressionistically, to sketch social situations that are characterized by, or that lack, decency and what it is for individuals to be well- or ill-mannered. Let me now attempt to say more precisely what decency might be.

WHAT IS DECENCY?

What I am referring to here as decency or good manners is but one aspect of the ethical life. It is that aspect concerned with attitudes toward, and treatment of, nonintimates with whom one comes into face-to-face contact. It is not, in other words, concerned with the individual's appropriate ethical attitude toward humanity at large or with the appropriate attitude toward, and treatment of, friends and intimates. Such attitudes are not rigidly compartmentalized, however: In a person's actual ethical life, there will be some overlap between the person's attitude toward, and treatment of, nonintimates and her treatment of her friends.

The attitude in question will be one of goodwill toward others and a concern for their welfare, which will often be expressed in the rituals of everyday life. These rituals include, for instance, greetings and farewells, the way apologies are made, the way regret, sympathy, congratulations, and the like are expressed. If we have the attitude of goodwill *and* we feel at home with the rituals for expressing it, we shall feel comfortable in the situation and feel that our behavior is sincere and authentic. The rituals will not be perceived as external constraints on our behavior but will indeed express how we feel. But there are less happy situations. In some situations we may not know the rituals and our behavior may be misinterpreted. The Bank of America, according to a recent British television program, is very conscious of these possibilities in its appraisal interviews. When an interviewer asks an employee how she feels about the goals she is expected to achieve in the coming

year, the interviewer expects a certain kind of response, typically perhaps the all-American response "No problem!" and may perhaps mis-
interpret the "I will try my best" of someone from a minority group as
not showing sufficient confidence and commitment. In international
contexts the possibilities for misunderstandings abound. Variations in
telephone manners (see "How the phone can cross wires," 1992) offer
many opportunities for offense. What happens when well-mannered
Britons and Italians, who think it appropriate to keep up a ceaseless flow
of talk, telephone Finns or Japanese, who think it polite to ponder what
has been said in silence?

In other situations we may behave *in accordance with* the rituals but
feel ill at ease, embarrassed, and self-conscious. This will characteristically be the case when we are in social groups where the rituals are different from those we are used to—a theme richly exploited in many
novels, plays, and films of the Yank at Oxford/Pygmalion genre. In those
cases, although we may, for instance, be anxious to show our concern
and so conduct ourselves in accordance with the rituals, it will not feel
to us like a sincere expression of concern. A doctoral student from South
Korea told me about his feelings of unease at greeting his supervisor in
the United States with the customary "Hi!" He knew that in the context
it was polite, but it felt wrong.

In putting the emphasis on rules and rituals in this way, it is important not to lose sight of two important ways in which decency is a
matter of going beyond the rules. It involves, on the one hand, not insisting on one's rights, giving people the benefit of the doubt, going the
extra mile. It involves an attitude, in other words, in which one's own
legitimate interests and concerns are not always given precedence even
when there might be some justification for doing so. Decency, also, on
the other hand, often involves giving other people more than just their
rights. Lieutenant Commander Nathan Jones of the U.S. Central Com-
mand in the Gulf War caught this aspect of decency in describing the
preparations that had been made to provide facilities for prisoners of
war better than those required by the Geneva Convention. According
to a report in *The Independent* at the time:

> "We are not only going to treat them humanely; we are going to treat them
> with decency and kindness," he said. "They will be treated better than
> before their capture." (Boggan, 1991)

Although Lieutenant Commander Jones's *words* aptly convey the
idea that decency involves giving people more than their rights, there
is perhaps a doubt as to whether this is in fact a case of pure decency.

Decent behavior proceeds from goodwill toward others, and here goodwill may well have been mixed with the motive of winning over the hearts and minds of the Iraqi soldiers and persuading them to surrender or desert. As such, it is at least decent behavior with a question mark over it. However, even if the behavior proceeds from unalloyed goodwill, this case suggests a further dimension to the notion of decency. So far the idea has been that it is an attitude that can characterize relationships between individuals, but institutions, too, can have codes of decency in behavior, which their individual members follow with varying degrees of commitment.

The quotation from Lieutenant Commander Jones perhaps also suggests that different areas of life have their own manners, their own code of decency. So the academic world of lectures, paper writing, and so on has its own forms of behavior to guide relations between nonintimates (see Palma's [1991] remarks about philosophical good manners), as does, say, the world of the theater or of industry. It would be a mistake to assume that these forms of behavior universally follow the same pattern, and it is important to bear this in mind as international collaboration increases in many spheres.

This discussion of decency has been centered, often explicitly, on the expression of certain attitudes in a democracy. In any society there will be some customary forms for the expression of what that society considers to be appropriate attitudes toward nonintimates. These customary forms will vary insofar as different societies will cherish different overarching ideals about what is important in social life. In a hierarchical society, for instance, decent behavior and good manners will have much to do with the appropriate recognition of others' status and ways of "saving face" when mistakes are made. In democratic societies, too, there will be forms of behavior that involve recognition of others and ways of avoiding embarrassment when things go awry. In democratic societies, however, the emphasis will characteristically be on forms that embody the recognition of others as equals and encourage the friendly social intercourse that Brogan was aware of in the atmosphere of the small town in Illinois. It is this, what one might call the expression of *democratic decency*, which is the focus of this exploratory treatment.

Decency, then, as I am concerned with it in a democratic society, is a matter of having an attitude of goodwill toward nonintimates, which will be expressed in different ways in different groups. It will often involve not insisting on one's rights and giving other people more than is due to them. It is an attitude expressed by individuals in their behavior, but institutions, too, can have codes of decency to guide their members' behavior.

THE EXPRESSION OF DECENCY

In contemporary societies, including multicultural ones, that aspire to be democratic, the customs and habits of decent behavior will vary between different social groups. I have already touched on this point and the phenomenon of the ignorance of, or poor mastery of, the customs of decency and its exploitation in comedy. Not knowing what decency demands—in the way, for instance, of punctuality, gratitude, and what will not embarrass others—is always a difficult position to be in because one knows that, despite one's best intentions, there is a strong chance that one will do the wrong thing. Randell Jarrell (1987) captured the extreme feelings that can occur when one is faced with unfamiliar manners when he said, "To Americans English manners are far more frightening than none at all" (p. 21).

Enterprises in contemporary societies, of which the Bank of America is just one example, have an interest in creating an atmosphere in which their employees and clients feel at ease. It is not surprising, then, that they are willing to spend money on courses in interpersonal skills. Such courses are often disparaged, since it is claimed that they teach arts of dissembling in order to manipulate people. Skills can, of course, always be put to evil ends, but should such courses be written off because they can be misused? They might be seen, more positively, as attempts to prevent misunderstandings between different groups by offering insight into their manners. For instance, teaching people to understand others' body language may prevent overhasty and false conclusions about others' intentions. They might also be seen as attempts to put a necessary brake on what might otherwise be an unrelenting pursuit of efficiency in that they create patterns of behavior which encourage people to treat others in a friendly way. Misgivings about courses in interpersonal skills and the like may still remain, however, in that at the heart of decency and good manners is the attitude of goodwill toward others, whereas the driving force behind courses in interpersonal skills is likely to be, at best, mixed with a desire for some other commercially oriented end.

WHAT IS WRONG WITH DECENCY?

The picture thus far has been of an attitude of goodwill toward others that seeks appropriate expression in behavior which others will understand and find agreeable. What possible objections could there be to such behavior?

Pope and Lowell seem to object to what is seen as the shallowness and superficiality of a life of decency. "Content to dwell in Decencies for ever" suggests a life conducted according to a set of external rules that are followed because they are the "done thing." This is life lived at the level of convention for its own sake. Decency would not be easy to defend if it meant this kind of conventional life, for such a life would lack authenticity. It would merely be an empty following of the rules. But decency is not an inauthentic mode of life, for the behavior of the decent person is animated by her desire to express her goodwill in an appropriate way.

This first objection can, then, be answered by reemphasising the authentic values of the life of decency. By contrast, the next cluster of objections challenges the values underlying the life of decency by drawing attention to values it neglects or does not sufficiently emphasize. It may be felt, for instance, that attention to others' feelings, and especially their self-esteem, is given too much importance in the life of decency to the neglect of values like honesty and integrity. It would be better if people were always told the truth about their contributions to meetings and so on. Similarly, attention to what justice demands may well mean that one must overstep the bounds of decency. In assertiveness courses, for instance, people are often encouraged not to fall in with what might be demanded by local good manners but firmly to stand up for neglected interests. Thus where current mores do not do justice to the interests of women, blacks, disabled people, and other groups, people are encouraged to challenge these.

That there are values other than those prominent in decency cannot be denied. But it need not be assumed that a concern for honesty and justice must always lead to a head-on clash with the values of decency. People with insight and imagination will often be able to behave decently while also being honest and making sure that rights are not infringed. Even when that is not possible, however, it does not follow that those other values of, for instance, honesty and justice, are *always* to be preferred to the concern for others at the heart of decency. When they should be so preferred is a matter for judgment.

The values of democratic decency remain, then, although, as we have seen, they may on some occasions, in the light of judgment, have to give way to the more pressing demands of justice or honesty. The development of such judgment is a matter for education.

DEMOCRATIC DECENCY AND THE SCHOOL

The Foreword to the British National Curriculum Council's (1990) *Education for Citizenship* tells us that democracy is one of the "values by which a civilized society is identified." If the foregoing account of the appropriate relationships among nonintimates in a democratic society is more or less on the right lines, it carries a powerful message for the school: If it wants to promote that value, as the document suggests it should, then it needs to pay attention to decency.

The school will most successfully teach decency if, in the main, it *shows* it rather than instructs in it. Describing how he first became aware of the intellectual virtues of patience, accuracy, economy, elegance, and style, Michael Oakeshott (1973) says that he owed his recognition of them

> to a Sergeant gymnastics instructor . . . not on account of anything he ever said, but because he was a man of patience, accuracy, economy, elegance and style. (p. 176)

And so it is with the values of democratic decency. For I would follow the line of argument developed by Oakeshott (1973) in "Learning and Teaching" to the conclusion that these will be most impressively conveyed through the *behavior* of members of the school.

As far as the school staff is concerned, it will not be simply a matter of their behavior *as individuals*: This will quite properly have different emphases according to the weighting they give to the different values embodied within decency. Institutions, as we noted, can also have their own codes of behavior, and therefore the behavior of individual members of the school staff in their roles *as teachers* in that institution will be very important. As a school staff, they will need to look explicitly at what the rules, customs, and expected patterns of behavior express so that they do not unwittingly offend against democratic decency. This applies not least to well-meaning attempts to "improve" the manners of children who come from backgrounds where the ritual expression of goodwill is simply different.

The more thorough the school's attention to detail, the more effective the education in democratic decency will be. Much of it, in the nature of the school, will occur through the different areas of the curriculum. For instance, English teachers often stress the importance of audience in writing and in this way remind their students that if a piece of writing is for public consumption, it needs to have certain qualities—like clarity—out of concern for the reader. It is not farfetched, I think, to say with Somerset Maugham (1951) that "to write good prose is an affair of good manners" (p. 25).

The school staff and the school's organization and ethos will, then, implicitly show decency. At times, however, teachers may need *explicitly* to focus their students' attention on its demands. This will be the case, for instance, with young children in elementary school who may need either to learn what is appropriate on a particular occasion or to have their memories prompted. Teachers may also have to encourage young children to appreciate that different forms of behavior, perhaps originating in different cultural traditions, can be just as much expressions of good-will as those they have learned. Adolescents may challenge their teach-ers on the importance of some aspects of decent behavior either verbally or by their flouting of the rules. They may want to claim that the interests of justice or personal independence demand that decency take a back seat. In all cases teachers will need to have reflected on what is involved in democratic decency. With young children they can, then, be properly insistent on forms of behavior that are expressive of goodwill toward others without feeling that they are, for instance, simply imposing "white middle-class values." With adolescents they will be able to encourage them to disentangle the conflicting values involved in their protest and help them to come to a view about how they should be weighted.

These kinds of explicit treatment of decency with young children and adolescents are very much in the nature of running repairs: A par-ticular incident in the day-to-day life of the school requires the teacher to draw attention to what decency demands. As children's understand-ing of their society develops, however, there is a place for a more reflec-tive treatment of the place of decency in social life—not least to counter the danger of parochialism already noted. There is a strong temptation to believe that the habits and customs we have grown up with are the only suitable expression of goodwill toward others without probing that thought too deeply. When we learn about or encounter other habits, they may seem to us wrong or at least inferior to the ones we are familiar with. As Hume (1959) remarks:

> Many of the forms of breeding are arbitrary and casual, but the thing ex-pressed by them is still the same. A Spaniard goes out of his own house before his guest, to signify that he leaves him master of all. In other coun-tries, the landlord walks out last, as a common mark of deference and regard. (p. 244)

Many areas of the curriculum—modern languages, geography, history, English—as well as, in many cases, the presence of diverse cultural groups in the classroom itself will provide opportunities to explore the expression of common values in different local mores.

The importance of the ethos of a school and the quality of the rela-tionships among its members has been emphasized throughout this book. This chapter suggests that the idea of democratic decency should inform the character of that ethos and those relationships, as well as itself being a subject for critical reflection in the curriculum. Without it, any education for citizenship is incomplete.

CHAPTER 9

Concluding Remarks

The preceding discussions of hope, social confidence, courage, self-esteem, self-respect, friendship, trust, honesty, and decency as aspects of citizenship education are in several ways just the beginning of work in this area. For a start, in every case the treatment of those topics here has raised further questions—and these have been some of the most intriguing as well as the most intractable—that have been left unanswered. Not only that, but it seems to me that there are more dispositions to be explored that have a very direct relevance to the life of democratic citizens. While I was finishing this work, studies of loyalty (Fletcher, 1993), gratitude (McConnell, 1993), patience (Callan, 1993), and anger in public life (Nussbaum, 1994) were published. All of them have obvious links with these discussions. Others, too—like mercy— suggest themselves.

In a very different sense, this book is just a beginning of work in this area, in that, as I suggested in Chapter 1, these attributes need to be imaginatively considered by practitioners in relation to the particular contexts in which they are working. Take hope, for instance. Does it make sense to talk of engendering democratic hopes in young children in elementary school? And, if so, won't that be very different from the task facing the teacher of some already politically cynical young adolescents if she is to encourage them to entertain democratic hopes? Similarly, helping children to resolve the difficulties that arise in their friendships will call on very different teacherly skills in elementary school and the high school class. In my experience, too, discussion of these topics with students from different ethnic backgrounds will often elicit mention of a value that is more dominant in their experience than in the mainstream culture. Discussions of friendship with Greek students have revealed the immensely high place given to hospitality in some cultures, so high a place that it can justify one's getting into serious debt. An Indian student once indicated a different perspective on responsibility, one in which passively bearing burdens was at least as highly valued as assertively taking charge of affairs. Again, as much of the work in this study shows (for instance, Rorty's treatment of courage and Baier's of trust), women philosophers will often highlight particular aspects of some values, thus revealing a more many-sided value than some interpretations might suggest. Exploring the various insights thrown up by such discussions may change one's understanding of the virtues and their interrelationship. It may also help one to understand the values, priorities, and projects of other men and women from other traditions and ethnic groups. Such explorations need to be at the heart of education in a democratic society.

Finally, if democratic dispositions are as important in the life of a society as this study has argued, and if their development in education is the complex matter suggested, a new approach is needed in the area of educational policy. All too often governments all over the world see moral and citizenship education as unproblematic—something teachers can easily take in their stride as they give their major attention to the really important tasks of teaching math, science, and history. These discussions reveal the inadequacy of that view by illustrating some of the ethical complexities in this area and the careful judgment and constant attention that teachers and school communities have to devote to moral and citizenship education if students are to be helped to become responsible and active democratic citizens. But understanding of the issues and careful judgment about how to create a school and classroom environment in which democratic dispositions can be fostered—whether in an inner city, a leafy suburb, or a remote rural community—are not something that can be sorted out by teachers on the drive or bus ride to school. Teachers need time to reflect on these issues and the delicate matter of applying them to the educational situations in which they find themselves. Just as important, they need time to discuss with colleagues how the school community should be structured as an institution in which students can become hopeful, confident, courageous, honest, self-respecting citizens with appropriate self-esteem, knowing how, when, and whom to trust and distrust and able to experience the rich pleasures of friendship.

REFERENCES
INDEX
ABOUT THE AUTHOR

References

Andrews, S. (1989). The ignominy of raised hands. In C. Harber & R. Meighan (Eds.), *The democratic school: Educational management and the practice of democracy* (pp. 146–156). Ticknell, United Kingdom: Education Now.

Aristotle. (1984). *The complete works of Aristotle* (J. Barnes, Ed.). Princeton, NJ: Princeton University Press.

Bacon, F. (1985). *The essays.* Harmondsworth, U.K.: Penguin. (Original work published 1625)

Baier, A. (1986). Trust and antitrust. *Ethics, 96,* 231–260.

Baier, A. C. (1990). Why honesty is a hard virtue. In O. Flanagan & A. O. Rorty (Eds.), *Identity, character and morality* (pp. 259–282). Cambridge, MA: MIT Press.

Barnes, J. (1981). *Metroland.* London: Robin Clark.

Barnes, J. (1987). *Staring at the sun.* London: Pan.

Bellah, R. N., Madsen, R., Sullivan, W. M., Swidler, A., & Tipton, S. M. (1985). *Habits of the heart: Individualism and commitment in American life.* Berkeley: University of California Press.

Bloch, Ernst (1986). *The principle of hope.* Oxford, U.K.: Blackwell.

Blum, L. (1980). *Friendship, altruism and morality.* London: Routledge.

Boggan, S. (1991, February 25). 10,000 POWs begin the flood that could slow the assault. *The Independent* (London), p. 1.

Bok, S. (1978). *Lying: Moral choice in public and private life.* Hassocks, United Kingdom: Harvester.

Bok, S. (1984). *Secrets: On the ethics of concealment and revelation.* Oxford, United Kingdom: Oxford University Press.

Brookner, A. (1982). *Look at me.* London: Triad Grafton.

Callan, E. (1993). Patience and courage. *Philosophy, 68*(266), 523–539.

Carr, W. (1991). Education for democracy? A philosophical analysis of the national curriculum. *Journal of the Philosophy of Education, 25*(2), 183–191.

Carson, M. (1989). *Sucking sherbert lemons.* London: Black Swan.

Casey, J. (1990). *Pagan virtue: An essay in ethics.* Oxford, United Kingdom: Clarendon.

Chang, J. (1993). *Wild swans: Three daughters of China.* London: Flamingo.

Chesterton, G. K. (1919). *Heretics.* London: John Lane, The Bodley Head.

Cicero. (1971). Laelius: On friendship. In M. Grant (trans.), *On the good life* (pp. 172–227). Harmondsworth, United Kingdom: Penguin.

Colegate, I. (1988). *Deceits of time.* London: Hamish Hamilton.

Cooper, J. (1980). Aristotle on friendship. In A. O. Rorty (Ed.), *Essays on Aristotle's ethics* (pp. 301–340). London: University of California Press.

Cox C., Douglas-Home, J., Marks, J., Norcross, L., & Scruton, R. (1986). *Whose schools? A radical manifesto.* London: Hillgate Group.

Crick, B., & Porter, A. (1978). *Political education and political literacy.* Harlow, U.K.: Longman.

Dewey, J. (1963). *Democracy and education.* New York: Macmillan. (Original work published 1916)

Dunn, J. (1988). Trust and political agency. In D. Gambetta (Ed.), *Trust: Making and breaking cooperative relations* (pp. 73–93). Oxford, U.K.: Basil Blackwell.

Dworkin, R. (1977). *Taking rights seriously.* London: Duckworth.

Dworkin, R. (1985). *A matter of principle.* London: Harvard University Press.

Elliott, R. K. (1989). Self-knowledge and education. In P. White (Ed.), *Personal and social education: Philosophical perspectives* (pp. 34–53). London: Kogan Page.

Ellmann, R. (Ed.). (1975). *Selected letters of James Joyce.* London: Faber & Faber.

Fielding, M. (1985). Celebration—valuing what we do. In R. Blatchford (Ed.), *Managing the secondary school* (pp. 170–185). London: Bell & Hyman.

Fisher, M. (1990). *Personal love.* London: Duckworth.

Fletcher, G. P. (1993). *Loyalty: An essay on the morality of relationships.* Oxford, U.K.: Oxford University Press.

Foot, P. (1981). *Virtues and vices.* Oxford, U.K.: Blackwell.

Forster, E. M. (1976). *Two cheers for democracy.* Harmondsworth, U.K.: Penguin.

Gambetta, D. (1988). *Trust: Making and breaking cooperative relations.* Oxford, U.K.: Basil Blackwell.

Giroux, H. (1989). *Schooling for democracy: Critical pedagogy in the modern age.* London: Routledge.

Godfrey, J. (1987). *A philosophy of human hope.* Dordrecht, The Netherlands: Martinus Nijhoff.

Greene, G. (1971). *The heart of the matter.* London: Penguin.

Hargreaves, D. (1982). *The challenge for the comprehensive school.* London: Routledge & Kegan Paul.

Haydon, G. (1987). Towards a framework of commonly accepted values. In G. Haydon (Ed.), *Education for a pluralist society: Philosophical perspectives on the Swann report* (pp. 25–37) (Bedford Way Paper). London: Institute of Education, University of London.

Hayward, J. (Ed.). (1983). *Penguin book of English verse.* Harmondsworth, U.K.: Penguin Books Ltd.

Highsmith, P. (1977). *Edith's diary.* London: Heinemann.

Houston, B. (1993). Speaking candidly. In *Proceedings of the Philosophy of Education Society 1993* (pp. 110–113). Urbana: University of Illinois.

How the phone can cross wires. (1992, February 23). *The Independent on Sunday.*

Hume, D. (1959). *Hume's moral and political philosophy* (H. Aiken, Ed.). New York: Hafner.

Jarrell, R. (1987). *Pictures from an institution*. London: Faber.

Jones, M. (1987). Prejudice. In G. Haydon (Ed.), *Education for a pluralist society: Philosophical perspectives on the Swann report* (Bedford Way Paper, pp. 39–56). London: Institute of Education, University of London.

Kant, I. (1949). *Critique of practical reason and other writings in moral philosophy* (L. B. White, ed. and Trans.). Chicago: University of Chicago Press.

Kant, I. (1963). *Lectures on ethics* (L. Infield, Trans.). New York: Harper & Row.

Kekes, J. (1989). *Moral tradition and individuality*. Princeton, N.J.: Princeton University Press.

Kennedy, J. F. (1956). *Profiles in courage*. New York: Harper & Row.

Kenny, A. (1992). *The metaphysics of mind*. Oxford, U.K.: Oxford University Press.

Lane, R. E. (1982). Government and self-esteem. *Political theory*, 10(1), 5–31.

Levi, P. (1987). *If this is a man*. London: Abacus.

Lowell, R. (1964). During fever. In *Life Studies*. New York: Farrar, Strauss & Giroux.

Luhmann, N. (1979). *Trust and power*. Chichester, U.K.: Wiley.

MacIntyre, A. (1984). *After virtue* (2nd ed.). Notre Dame, IN: University of Notre Dame Press.

Malamud, B. (1968). *A new life*. Harmondsworth, U.K.: Penguin.

Marcel, G. (1967). Desire and hope. In N. Lawrence & D. O'Connor (Eds.), *Readings in existential phenomenology* (pp. 278–286). Englewood Cliffs, NJ: Prentice-Hall.

Marquez, G. G. (1988). *Love in the time of cholera*. London: Cape.

Martin, J. R. (1993). Curriculum and the mirror of knowledge. In R. Barrow and P. White (Eds.), *Beyond liberal education: Essays in honour of Paul H. Hirst* (pp. 107–128). London: Routledge.

Maugham, W. S. (1951). *The summing up*. London: Heinemann.

McConnell, T. (1993). *Gratitude*. Philadelphia: Temple University Press.

McGurk, H. (1987). *What next*. London: Economic and Social Research Council.

McLaughlin, T. H. (1992). Citizenship, diversity and education: A philosophical perspective. *Journal of Moral Education*, 21(3), 235–250.

Michell, G. (1990). Women and lying: A pragmatic and semantic analysis of telling it slant. In A. Y. al-Hibri & M. A. Simons (Eds.), *Hypatia reborn* (pp. 175–191). Bloomington: Indiana University Press.

Moseley, J. (1993). *Turn your school around*. Wisbech, U.K.: Learning Development Aids.

Nagel, T. (1979). The fragmentation of values. In *Mortal questions* (pp. 128–141). Cambridge, United Kingdom: Cambridge University Press.

National Curriculum Council. (1990). *Education for citizenship*. London: Her Majesty's Stationery Office.

Nielsen, K. (1985). *Equality and liberty: A defense of radical egalitarianism*. Totowa, NJ: Rowan & Allanheld.

Nozick, R. (1974). *Anarchy, state and utopia*. Oxford, U.K.: Blackwell.

Nussbaum, M. (1986). *The fragility of goodness*. Cambridge, U.K.: Cambridge University Press.

Nussbaum, M. (1994). *The therapy of desire: Theory and practice in Hellenistic ethics*. Princeton, NJ: Princeton University Press.

Oakeshott, M. (1973). Learning and teaching. In R. S. Peters (Ed.), *The concept of education* (pp. 156–176). London: Routledge.

O'Hear, P., & White, J. (1991). *A national curriculum for all: Laying the foundations for success* (IPPR Education and Training Paper No. 6). London: Institute for Public Policy Research.

Palma, A. B. (1991). Philosophizing. *Philosophy, 66*(255), 41–51.

Power, V. (1993, August 12). Given room to be themselves. *The Independent* (London).

Rawls, J. (1973). *A theory of justice*. Oxford, U.K.: Oxford University Press.

Rawls, J. (1985). Justice as fairness: Political not metaphysical. *Philosophy and Public Affairs, 14*, 223–251.

Rawls, J. (1993). *Political liberalism*. New York: Columbia University Press.

Raz, J. (1986). *The morality of freedom*. Oxford, U.K.: Clarendon.

Rorty, A. R. (1986). The two faces of courage. *Philosophy, 61*(236), 151–171.

Sabini, J., & Silver, M. (1982). *Moralities of everyday life*. Oxford, U.K.: Oxford University Press.

Sachs, D. (1982). How to distinguish self-respect from self-esteem. *Philosophy and Public Affairs, 10*, 346–360.

Sher, G. (1989). *Desert*. Princeton, NJ: Princeton University Press.

Shklar, J. (1984). *Ordinary vices*. London: Harvard University Press.

Singer, I. B. (1990). A peephole in the gate. In *The death of Methuselah* (pp. 93–120). London: Penguin.

Smith, R. (1985). *Freedom and discipline*. London: Allen & Unwin.

Spiecker, B. (1990). Forms of trust in education and development. *Studies in Philosophy and Education, 10*(2), 157–164.

Taylor, C. (1985). *Philosophy and the human sciences: Philosophical Papers*. Cambridge, U.K.: Cambridge University Press.

UNESCO. (1983). *Course of study for elementary schools in Japan*. Tokyo: Author.

Wallace, J. D. (1986). *Virtues and vices*. London: Cornell.

Walton, D. N. (1986). *Courage: A philosophical investigation*. London: University of California Press.

Walzer, M. (1983). *Spheres of justice: A defence of pluralism and equality*. Oxford, U.K.: Martin Robertson.

Warnock, M. (1986). The education of the emotions. In D. Cooper (Ed.), *Education, values and mind* (pp. 172–187). London: Routledge.

White, J. (1987). The quest for common values. In G. Haydon (Ed.), *Education for a pluralist society: Philosophical perspectives on the Swann report* (pp. 13–24). (Bedford Way Paper). London: Institute of Education, University of London.

White, J., & White, P. (1986). Education, liberalism and human good. In D. Cooper (Ed.), *Education, values and mind* (pp. 149–171). London: Routledge.

White, P. (1973). Education, democracy and the public interest. in R. S. Peters (Ed.), *Philosophy of education* (pp. 217–238). Oxford, U.K.: Oxford University Press.

White, P. (1983). *Beyond domination: An essay in the political philosophy of education*. London: Routledge.

White, P. (1988). The playground project: A democratic learning experience. In H. Lauder & P. Brown (Eds.), *Education: In search of a future* (pp. 192–206). Lewes, U.K.: Falmer.

Williams, B. (1978). Politics and moral character. In S. Hampshire (Ed.), *Public and private morality* (pp. 55–73). Cambridge, U.K.: Cambridge University Press.

Williams, B. (1981). Conflicts of values. In *Moral luck* (pp. 71–82). Cambridge, U.K.: Cambridge University Press.

Williams, B. (1985). *Ethics and the limits of philosophy*. London: Fontana.

Williams, B. (1987). The primacy of dispositions. In G. Haydon (Ed.), *Education and values: The Richard Peters Lectures* (pp. 56–65). London: Institute of Education, University of London.

Williams, R. (1979). *Modern tragedy*. London: Verso.

Wilson, J. (1987). *A preface to morality*. London: Macmillan.

Wringe, C. (1992). The ambiguities of education for active citizenship. *Journal of Philosophy of Education*, 26(1), 29–38.

Index

Aristotle, 38, 40–46, 51, 53, 71
Austen, J., 50

Bacon, F., 43–45
Baier, A., 2, 52, 53, 55, 56, 68, 72, 88
Barnes, Julian, 17, 18, 70, 72
Bellah, R. N., et al., 38
Bloch, E., 9
Blum, L., 38–39, 48, 50
Bok, S., 48–49, 52, 55, 69
Brogan, D., 80, 83
Brookner, A., 78

Callan, E., 88
Candor, 70–74
Carr, W., 25
Carson, M., 47–48
Casey, J., 81
Chang, J., 51
Chesterton, G. K., 8, 9
Cicero, 44, 51
Colegate, I., 40
Constant, B., 68
Cooper, J., 42
Courage, 3, 16–25
    analysis of, 16–20
    and education for democracy, 20–
        25
Cox, C., et al., 66
Crick, B., 25

Decency, 4, 78–87
    analysis of, 79–83
    and civic education, 85–87
    objections to, 84–85

Democracy, 11–12
    procedures of, 1, 8
Dewey, J., 1
Dispositions. *See also entries under
    specific dispositions*
    defined, 2
    democratic, 1–7
    ethical, 2
    fostering, 5
    understanding, 6
Dunn, J., 57, 58, 59
Dworkin, R., 3, 28

Education for citizenship, 1, 20–25,
    75–76, 78, 85–87, 89
    critiques of in the UK, 25
Elliott, R. K., 75
Ellmann, R., 55
Ethical confidence. *See* Social
    confidence.

Fielding, M., 37
Fisher, M., 71
Fletcher, G. P., 88
Foot, P., 16
Forster, E. M., 4, 5
Friendship, 4, 38–51
    Aristotle's types of friendship, 40–
        42
    downside of friendship, 42
    fostering friendship, 46–51
    value of friendship, 43–46

Gambetta, 53, 59
Giroux, H., 10

Godfrey, J., 9
Greene, G., 10

Hargreaves, D., 32
Haydon, G., 32, 37
Highsmith, P., 17–18
Hillgate Group, 66
Honesty, 4, 66–77. *See also* Candor;
    Lying; Stealing
  obstacles to, 72
  and political education, 75
Hope, 3, 8–15
  social hopes, 8–12
  social hopes and Christianity, 9–
    11
  social hopes and liberal
    democracy, 11–12
  social hopes and Marxism, 9–
    11
Houston, B., 74
Hume, D., 80, 81, 87

Jarrell, R., 84
Jones, M., 37
Joyce, J., 55
Justice, 3

Kant, I., 68–69, 70, 71
Kekes, J., 11, 80
Kennedy, John F., 20, 24
Kenny, A., 2

Lane, R., 28
Levi, P., 22
Locke, J., 53
Lowell, R., 78, 84
Luhmann, N., 52, 53, 55, 56, 58, 59,
    62
Lying, 66–70

McConnell, T., 88
McGurk, H., 25
MacIntyre, A., 2, 16
McLaughlin, T., 25
Malamud, B., 46

Marcel, G., 9–11
Marquez, G. G., 40
Martin, J. R., 32
Maugham, S., 86
Mitchell, G., 70
Montaigne, M. de, 51
Moseley, J., 37

Nagel, T., 11
Nielsen, K., 30, 32
Nozick, R., 28, 30, 32
Nussbaum, M., 2, 40, 88

Oakeshott, M., 86
O'Hear, P., 32

Palma, A. B., 83
Personal autonomy, 3
Plato, 1, 53
Pope, A., 78, 84
Porter, A., 25
Power, V., 37

Racism, 73
Rawls, J., 3, 26, 27, 30
Raz, J., 3
Richardson, S., 8
Rorty, A. O., 2, 3, 16, 19, 22, 26,
    88
Rorty, R., 10
Rousseau, J.-J., 1

Sabini, J., 48
Sachs, D., 26, 30
School
  and courage, 20–25
  and decency, 85–87
  and the fostering of friendship,
    46–51
  and honesty, 72–77
  as an institution, 5
  as a multicultural institution, 5–6,
    31, 62, 88
  and the promotion of social
    confidence, 13–14

and self-esteem, 30–37
and self-respect, 28–32
and trust, 60–65
Self-deception, 74
Self-esteem, 3
    defined and distinguished from
        self-respect, 26–28
    and education, 33–37
    fostering of, 32–37
    problems with, 32–33
    tensions between self-respect and,
        30–32
Self-knowledge, 74
Self-respect, 3
    defined and distinguished from
        self-esteem, 26–28
    and democratic values, 28
    and education, 33–37
    fostering of, 29–30
    and institutions, 28–29
    tensions between self-esteem and,
        30–32
Sexism, 70, 73
Sher, G., 67
Shklar, J., 58
Silver, M., 48
Singer, B. I., 56
Smith, R., 36
Social confidence, 3, 12–13
    and the school, 13–14
    and trust, 57

Spiecker, B., 60
Stealing, 66–67

Taylor, C., 3
Teacher, art of, 6, 7
Thomas, L., 26
Tolerance, 3
Trust, 4, 52–65
    defined, 53–54
    and distrust, 58–60
    personal trust, 55–57, 64–65
    and the school, 60–65
    and school ethos, 60–63
    trust in institutions, 57
    understanding social trust and
        distrust, 63

Veracity, 67

Wallace, J., 16
Walton, D. N., 20
Walzer, M., 3, 30
Warnock, M., 8, 12
White, J., 32, 37, 46
White, P., 1, 14, 46, 79
Williams, B., 2, 3, 11, 12, 22, 57, 69,
    75–76
Williams, R., 10
Wilson, J., 40
Woolf, V., 35
Wringe, C., 25

About the Author

Patricia White is a Research Fellow in Philosophy of Education at the Institute of Education, University of London. Her publications include *Beyond Domination: An Essay in the Political Philosophy of Education* (Routledge, 1983), *Personal and Social Education: Philosophical Perspectives* (editor) (Kogan Page, 1989), *Beyond Liberal Education: Essays in Honour of Paul H. Hirst* (editor with Robin Barrow) (Routledge, 1993) as well as many papers on ethical and political aspects of philosophy of education.

She is currently Chair of the Philosophy of Education Society of Great Britain, a fellow of the American Philosophy of Education Society, and a member of Women in Philosophy.